BASEBALL CROSSWORDS

GAME 2   ENTER GATE D

SEAT 24

SECTION   ROW   SEAT

This portion must

Ticket $5
Tax $0.5

RAIN CHECK

AMAZON REVIEWS
ARE APPRECIATED

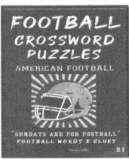

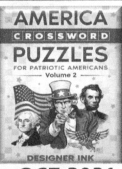

MORE ON PG 118

CLUE HELPERS

BASEBALL
GAME ON

Abbr - Abbreviation
(short) - shortened word
"word" - Focus word, AKA, or quoted
pl - plural version of clue
sl - Singular version of clue
(slang) - Less known, slang or urban
( ) important clarification e.g. year

(3wd) # of words in answer
AKA - Also Known As
NN - Nick Name
___ - Fill in the blank
No Spaces in Mult. Word answer
UPPER CASE - Acronyms
USA and **UK/CAN** English

SOLUTIONS PG 104

Find an error? Email us: Designerinkbooks@gmail.com

Across

1. MLB's "suspect" political posturing, 2020
5. 9th of a game's innings, unless tied
9. Tigers Catcher #13 Eric
14. Brewers Catcher #9 Manny
15. Twins Pitcher #82 Bailey
16. Cubs most hits: 2995
17. Similar to the shape of a baseball
18. Royals Mng 1980-81, 127W-105L
19. Phillies Pitcher #60 Ramón
20. Drafted AKA
22. Tampa Bay Rays NN
23. Astros City
25. Threw MLB's ceremonial 1st pitch 1950
29. Active players are said to be. Also, pre marriage
34. WS shown this way is not the same
35. Baseball, the national ___ime
37. Player's wives animal-like descriptor
38. Gamblers make on a game
39. Player assessment, determines their
40. Team jerseys
41. Ump changes a ball w this damage
42. Degree type of many college players
43. Orioles Catcher #28 Severino
44. Holds jock on
46. Each player is one
47. Source of wood for baseball bat
50. Players AKA
54. Nationals Infielder # 5 Josh
59. Poor team's request to league
60. Concession fountain drink
61. "Rake" the infield dirt
62. A zero on the scoreboard, egg
63. Diamond Backs territory (short)
64. Billings American Legion Baseball
65. Great hero like "___ Baseball 2020" on PS4
66. Braves St. Pitcher #19 Huascar
67. American Professional Baseball Assoc.

Down

1. Montreal Expos NN
2. Stadium on game day, a bee ___ of activity
3. Methodical coach
4. Pro baseball participants
5. Indians most stolen bases, 450, Kenny
6. Astros Pitcher #66 Bryan
7. MLB chew and spit sunflower food
8. Attempt a steal
9. Reds P w most SO to walk: 3.187
10. Trade rumors, often ___ ymous
11. Coaches helper (short)
12. 1998 NL MVP, Sammy
13. Baseball HOFer "Slaughter", Bradsher
21. 1st S. Korean in MLB ___ Ho Park, 1994-2010
22. April, Opening
24. MLB "checks" for PEDs
25. To switch a player's side
26. 2020 MLB has 10 active - Ol Miss alum
27. Tigers St. Pitcher #62 José
28. New York Mets NN
30. "Post" game
31. Game "details"
32. TV broadcast talent source
33. Royals Outfielder #1 Jarrod
35. Shallow OF, called a short ___
36. Reds Pitcher #77 Warren
39. Submarine pitch, side arm below this
43. Teammate AKA
45. Orioles Pitcher #66 Scott
46. Yankees Infielder #91 Oswald
48. Ego players to/in a coach's side
49. Popular baseball broadcast method of the past
50. Touches runner for the out
51. Fr. greats Felipe or Moises of MLB
52. Uniform belt goes through it
53. MLB teams can beat semi-pro teams with it
55. Inter County Baseball Assoc.
56. On a rope in the player's locker room
57. Official Major League Baseball
58. National Beep Baseball Assoc.
60. Star Spangled Banner, 2nd word

PUZZLE 1

1	2	3	4		5	6	7	8		9	10	11	12	13
14					15					16				
17					18					19				
20				21					22					
			23				24							
25	26	27	28				29			30	31	32	33
34					35	36				37				
38				39						40				
41				42					43					
44				45					46					
			47			48	49							
50	51	52	53			54				55	56	57	58
59					60					61				
62				63					64					
65				66					67					

Baseball Fact: "Take Me Out to the Ballgame" was written in 1908 by Jack Norworth and Albert von Tilzer, both of whom had never been to a baseball game

Across

1. Big players have plenty of it
5. Team w salary surplus, can for FA
11. Curveball AKA
12. Runner made it to 1B before the throw
14. Bat's fat end AKA
15. Player's bone injury
16. A too drunk, belligerent fan risks this
17. Pulled, not for poor performance
18. Player's girlfriend
19. Inherited Runs Allowed
20. Greatest Of All Time
21. Western Hemisphere Baseball League
22. True Earned Run Average
24. Team's standing ___ after losing streak
25. Orioles Pitcher #51 Fry
26. Star player, won't talk to teammates
27. Back up position player (short)
28. Credit card for tix, action
29. Where most fans watch the game
31. League's official approval (short)
32. Cross the plate
34. St. Louis Cardinals: Abbr
35. Pitchers stats
39. Player's energy source (sl, short)
40. Astros Outfielder #220 McCormick
41. Pitcher's shoulder muscle, sometimes injured (short)
42. North Royalton Baseball Boosters
43. Marlins Catcher #7 Sandy
44. Thornton Baseball Assoc.
45. Set high for team with stars
46. WS win fireworks noise
47. One who scores
50. Closer may ___ the game, 8th or 9th in.
52. Lists the scores (short)
53. Too small for new stadium
54. Feature of a baseball or golf shoe
55. Royals Infielder #49 Alberto
56. Players sunglass appearance

Down

1. Royals Mng 1986, 36W-38L record
2. Convince a player to sign. Also, fishing object
3. Standouts on the pitcher's mound
4. Uniform middle
5. All-Star game in July, for most players
6. Eat a lot at the game
7. MLB stat
8. 21 year Giant, "Master Melvin"
9. "Scuff up" the ball
10. Cal Ripken as a player, description
11. Yankees Pitcher #56 O'Day
13. Announcers do it all game, about the game
14. Trade rumors for press to eat up. Also, fish foods
15. Uniform buttons location
20. League award show
21. "Lined up" before using stadium's restroom
23. Pads must shock ___ to be effective
24. Common Umpire call
25. HOF Pee Wee Reese
28. Stadium divisions (short)
30. Baseball (slang)
31. A team acts as one, together. Also, Scottish group
32. Weak grounded base hit
33. 2013 AL Batting Champ
34. Reds Outfielder #4 Akiyama
36. Players on vacation, from baseball
37. Yankees Pitcher #84 Abreu
38. Houston Astros NN
40. Middle fielder
42. Newton Baseball Softball Assoc.
43. Tigers Pitcher #57 Alex
46. Fans have it deep for hometown team
47. Strikeout Rate
48. 5 MLB team state (short)
49. Stadium entrance is accessible
51. Signs a contract

PUZZLE 2

Baseball Fact: Early days baseballs were not cork centered. They contained such things as a rock to a walnut in the center

Across

1. Pro's Pre game attire, neck tie bundling
5. An Apple brand game streaming device
9. Caught Stealing Percentage, stat
14. Watching the game in the stadium
15. 2012 AL Gold Glove 2nd Base
16. Option for opening pitch, especially L.A.
17. Royals Infielder #27 Mondesí
19. Job is to get on base AKA ___ setter
20. Takes tickets at the door
21. Sharp triangular part of player's shoulder
22. Seen through a helmet hole
23. "Fast fwd" commercial, game recording
25. Red Sox St. Pitcher #43 Richards
29. Rub, to "develop" ball shine
33. Washington Team NN
34. A team's territory AKA
36. Tampa Bay Rays NN
37. Diamond Mind Baseball
38. Unpredictable variety of different pitches
40. Jersey wear and "tear"
41. Giants Closer, Wilson, famous for it
44. Half a teammate
45. Fox Sports Camera provider
46. Pitcher spit to ball flight
48. Stat column "organizing"
50. Home Plate AKA
52. # of ARZ Fall League teams
53. Puerto Rican Prof. Baseball League
56. 2 outs, baserunners will run ___
62. Single-A baseball AKA
63. Oakland Athletics NN
64. MLB Digest, periodical, is sold by the ___
65. Eager Beaver Baseball Assoc.
66. East Toronto Baseball Assoc.
67. Skills are tracked, formulated & prioritized
68. HR slang - ___ long distance
69. Tailgating BBQ cooking process

Down

1. Scully's voice heard on this LA radio
2. Mets Catcher #3 Tomás
3. A baseball is circular, a football is what?
4. Ticket sellers. Also, PBP guys
5. Concession dairy treat
6. An inning, of the total game
7. Players jump ___ loose balls
8. Closed overnight, stadium
9. Term for a team in a desirable position
10. "Anybody need tickets?"
11. Peters Township Baseball Assoc.
12. Typical Opening Day condition in the NE
13. Cleared from a game field, construction
18. Minnesota Twins Mascot
24. Royals city on a scoreboard
25. Pirates Outfielder #18 Ben
26. Completed plate appearance
27. Grass crew will, pre-game
28. Astros AAA team locale, state
30. Yankees Outfielder #99 Judge
31. Down by 1, so the runner on 3rd is what?
32. Sports athletes & writers award
33. North Delta Baseball Assoc.
35. Injury cart
39. ___ Seat License, such as seasons ticket
42. USA flag in stadium, ___ white & ___
43. Hit by pitch, like a power tool
45. Decade of MLB Expansion - 16 to 24 teams
47. Short Stop
49. Metal bat strike noise
51. Strong fire-man like throw (slang)
53. 2 cleats make 1
54. Revere Baseball Softball Assoc.
55. Baseball, the national ___ime
57. NorthWest Baseball Institute
58. Champions International Baseball Academy
59. Contract upping
60. Continental Amateur Baseball Association
61. MLB Comish AKA (slang)

PUZZLE 3

1	2	3	4		5	6	7	8		9	10	11	12	13
14					15					16				
17				18						19				
20										21				
			22					23	24					
	25	26				27	28		29			30	31	32
33					34			35		36				
37					38				39			40		
41			42	43		44					45			
46					47		48			49				
			50			51			52					
53	54	55				56	57	58				59	60	61
62						63								
64					65					66				
67					68					69				

Baseball Fact: Ken Griffey Sr. & Ken Griffey Jr. became the 1st father - son to play as MLB teammates for the 1990 SEA Mariners. On Sept 14, 1990, they hit B2B HRs, another father-son baseball first

Across

1. Players hearing, from too many loud crowds
5. Big Bad Baseball Annual
9. Nationals Catcher #38 Barrera
13. American Professional Baseball Assoc.
14. Indians Infielders #71 Gabriel
15. Stadium on game day, a bee ___ of activity
16. Blue Jays Pitcher #60 Ty
17. Stadiums are built on
18. 0-0 score
19. Baseball camp AKA
21. Team break-apart
23. A's most wild pitches: 87
24. 2005 NLCS MVP
25. Innings Played, stat
28. Camera controls
30. Injured easy when playing on turf
32. Diamondbacks on a scoreboard (short)
33. Concession food flavoring
37. Natural shade for players
39. Triple Crown College Baseball League
40. Royals Infielder #49 Alberto
42. Millionaires League Baseball
45. Slidell Bantam Baseball Association
46. MLB in the terms of league status
48. Coaches tell team to take one for cardio
49. Player knee support, brace AKA
51. Uniform wear and what?
54. Shutout AKA
55. Rangers Outfielder #3 Leody
59. 2009 Edgar Martinez Award
60. College ballers may be on free ___
62. 5x WS, 5x All-Star, '94 Cy Young "pylon" P
63. Star player may live on it, fall off of it
64. Live dog mascot nose noise
65. Eases hot summer day sunburn
66. Team owner may also be stadium ___ holder
67. Concession offerings
68. Phillies AAA team locale, state (short)

Down

1. Stats
2. The Yankees 27 WS wins is ___ in scale
3. American Baseball Coaches Assoc.
4. Tigers Pitcher #38 Alex
5. Nationals Pitcher #59 Ben
6. Stadium waste holder
7. Tigers Outfielders #60 Akil
8. A
9. Practice hones these skills
10. Red Sox to the Yankees
11. A ball game is a type of what?
12. Down to Farm League
14. Mets Outfielder #4 Albert
20. HOF Delahanty
22. Lost all games of series
25. Retired players get it, and want to return
26. Phillies St. Pitcher #27 Aaron
27. Sport bar's bright sign
29. Marlins City
31. League decides you won't be playing
34. Cape Cod Baseball League
35. Eager Beaver Baseball Assoc.
36. Hitter type w a high average, but low power
38. Tigers Outfielders #54 Hill
41. Turn back to 2nd
43. Yankees "NY"
44. Off center logo area on many jerseys
47. Yankees Pitcher #80 Luis
49. Avoid the tag action
50. Tigers Pitcher #57 Alex
52. HOF Arky Vaughan
53. Announcer summary of the game
54. Player did from serious injury
56. Actor Charlie Sheen as Ricky "Wild Thing" Vaughn in Major League movie
57. Trade rumors, often ___ ymous
58. Already watched game
61. To hit batter w ball, maybe intent

PUZZLE 4

Baseball Fact: The 1920s New York Yankees were the 1st team to wear numbers. They originally wore numbers matching the batting order. Babe Ruth hit third, so he was number 3.

Across

1. A's Infielder #4 Pinder
5. Stadium divisions (short)
9. Southwest Washington Adult Baseball League
14. Coach's nag. Also, a string instrument
15. Collegiate Baseball Umpires Assoc.
16. Roster "max"
17. Periods, eras or ___ in baseball
18. Needed after long, tiring game
19. Jays, Orioles or Cardinals mascot
20. Marlins most saves: 108
21. St. Louis Cardinals NN
23. "Hold" onto the bat
26. How trade rumors happen
27. Baseball training facility NN
30. Amateur Baseball Report
33. Marlins Infielder #24 Jesús
35. Tigers AAA Locale
36. Indians Pitcher #52 Nick
37. Common ball game & movie snack
39. Young player NN
40. Player makes it, direct to base
41. Like some batteries & baseball leagues
42. Mariners St. Pitcher #50 Erik
44. Sweat seen on player's head
45. MLB checks for PEDs
49. Aging player's foe
55. Player's Lid
56. Brewers Pitcher #52 Eric
57. Players non-baseball College purpose (short)
58. Ruth
59. Minnesota Twins Mascot
60. Pitchers between starts
61. State north of Rangers, Astros (short)
62. Concession food, comes w sauce
63. Youth Aluminum Baseball Bat
64. MLB film holder

Down

1. Indians Infielders #2 Yu
2. Mets Infielder #86 Jake
3. Stadium AKA
4. "Twin killings" in baseball: Abbr
5. Heal mark from turf skin injury
6. Eager Beaver Baseball Assoc.
7. Orioles most games, started: 40 (1970)
8. Mariners Pitcher #65 Casey
9. Fans rarely give a team this leeway
10. Women's International Baseball Assoc.
11. Reds Pitcher #50 Garrett
12. Jays, Orioles or Cardinals mascot
13. League corporate structure: Abbr
22. Original BAL Orioles, now this team as of 1903
24. Players need to, for understanding signs
25. Indians Pitcher #88 Maton
28. Marlins Pitcher #57 Hernández
29. Outside drinks into stadium
30. Players needing cardio go for ___
31. Grab a ___ , at the stadium concession
32. Season tix, holds that seat (short)
33. Player's skill btw AAA and the majors
34. Greater Niagara Baseball Assoc.
35. Error made by the right fielder
36. Stolen Base Attempts
37. Signs a contract
38. How often the Yankees win the WS
40. Start any sports league in 2020
43. Concession draft beer negative
44. Famous outside the S-Zone hitter, Yogi
46. Signal from a pitcher
47. Playoff teams displayed in it
48. Take a base, quickly
49. Blue Jays mascot movement
50. All American Baseball Alliance
51. An early week game day (short)
52. Pitcher's throw it, hot
53. Mendon Upton Senior Baseball
54. Elite Championship Tournament Baseball
58. Boston Rustlers (1911): Abbr

PUZZLE 5

Baseball Fact: The oldest baseball stadium still in use is Fenway Park, in Boston. The Park at #4 – Jersey Street opened on April 20th, 1912. I cost $650,000 ($17.4M in today's dollars) and seats 37,330+ fans.

Across

1. Team branded "Stuff-We-All-Get"
5. Brewers Infielder #21 Travis
9. 1st and 2nd
14. Has sports writing on it
15. Texarkana Arkansas Baseball Association
16. A's are threatening, again in 2021
17. Orioles St. Pitcher #45 Keegan
18. Visiting team's accommodations
19. "TV" satellite company, carries sports
20. Contract re-up'd
22. Marlins Pitcher #29 Nick
24. Action to get names on trophy
25. Most players retire for this reason
26. Old stadiums like OAK haven't done it well
27. Players very first league
32. Orioles Pitcher #68 Wells
34. Practice warm-up exercise (short)
35. Nationals Pitcher #59 Braymer
36. WS time (short)
37. 1992 ALCS MVP
41. To hit a batter (slang)
44. Looked for pitch, got it
46. Team practice for upcoming game (short)
47. Orioles Infielder #14 Ruiz
48. Currently outscoring opponent
52. Indians Infielders #84 Ernie
56. Big source of revenue for MLB
57. Shoe tighteners
58. Cola sponsor
60. Bell, that sponsors the All-star Legends
61. AB
62. Twins Pitcher #82 Bailey
63. East Toronto Baseball Assoc.
64. Contracts
65. Banana stalk (bat slang), ___ w bad wood
66. Pitcher's shoulder muscle injury (short)

Down

1. Utility bench player
2. Sleepy fans after big play
3. HGH, is for anti what?
4. Public type watching ball game
5. White Sox Pitcher #53 Jonathan
6. L or R e.g. batting
7. American Baseball Network
8. Cubs NLCS G6 fan catch attempt, MLB ruled it ___ interference
9. Start any sports league in 2020
10. Among pros
11. Pitcher's arm may be, post-game
12. Records are for the best ___
13. Stadium division (short)
21. Pro baller can have a high one
23. Night games need this power (short)
28. HOF Bullet Rogan
29. Nationals Pitcher #60 Joan
30. Concession ice cream, action
31. Stadium parking place
32. Vision to watch game
33. Braves St. Pitcher #19 Huascar
35. Non playoff team efforts. Also, over-ripe fruit
38. HOF Martín Dihigo
39. Cops taking away drunk fans
40. A champion's time, ruling over team-league
41. Practice helps, for game
42. Fielders attempt at a high hit ball
43. After refreshing MLB.com
45. MLB, online
46. Where a bet goes
49. Player after blatant bad call
50. New England Collegiate Baseball League
51. Players after a win, brag
52. Yanks finish with winning record? Iron ___
53. Swing and a miss....batter is, most times
54. East Coast Baseball Academy
55. Tailgating purpose, besides beer
59. Opponents' Batting Average

PUZZLE 6

Baseball Fact: The most stolen base is second base.

Across

1. Lose the large point lead
5. National Fantasy Baseball Championship
9. Coaching duration
13. Players travel in it
14. A team's territory AKA
15. Houston Senior Baseball Assoc.
16. Multiple 12 packs of balls
17. Tailgating purpose, besides beer
18. RBI triple
19. Player roster
20. Angered fan response
21. Teams on west and east
22. Term for a "No-swing strikeout"
24. 50-50 winner decided by
26. Soda and beer found here
29. Pitch to the close side of batter
33. OutField Assists
36. Gatorade electrolytes may prevent
38. Nationals Infielder #7 Turner
39. Comish who launched interleague play
41. Paid player (short)
42. Stadium and dugout tops
43. Pitch hits batter, w intent (slang)
44. Pitch right down the middle
46. Yankees on a scoreboard
47. AB
49. A mark made on telestrator
51. 2nd string players (short)
53. OT makes the game time
57. From your wall to TV, gets you ESPN
60. Salary deposit place (short)
63. Name of squad type for evaluation
64. Cubs NLCS G6 fan interf., player Moises
65. Many an extra come to training camp (short)
66. Players #1 familiar supporters
67. Place with the players lockers
68. HOF inductees (short)
69. Red Sox Pitcher #31 Austin
70. A Cubs concern in early season (short)
71. North Seattle Baseball Assoc.
72. Players vision correction tool

Down

1. Orioles most triples: 12 (1967)
2. Texas team logo design possibility
3. ___ three inning (all out)
4. Rangers Pitcher #63 Benjamin
5. ID on jersey
6. Baseball's low-cost agency
7. Giants Closer, Wilson, famous for it
8. Indians Pitcher #47 Quantrill
9. Pitcher ___ the Catcher, repeatedly
10. East Side Baseball Assoc.
11. RBI single
12. Angels Infielder #23 Thaiss
13. Portland City League Baseball
20. Shared Shea with Mets, 1964-83
21. SS Banner, 3rd word
23. Jersey caught on a buckle. Also, catch
25. Stadium beer glass edge
27. MLB HQ mtg, by ___ only: Abbr
28. 2011 NL Gold Glove Outfielder
30. Cal Ripken Jr. is this Man
31. Comeback team will do to the odds
32. Making it as a pro baller is anything but
33. Ontario Senior Baseball Assoc.
34. Players are above 6, usually
35. Angels AA team, state (short)
37. What is under the grass field
40. Trouble getting hits (3wd)
42. Home of Nevada's minor-league Aces
44. Star Spangled Banner
45. Each Savannah Bananas player wore one in 2018 St. Patrick's Day game
48. Early in the week game day (short)
50. 9 innings of a game
52. Thrown overhead of a player (slang)
54. White Sox Infielder #75 Sheets
55. Multiple team VPs, presidents (short)
56. All should do for the anthem
57. Injury vehicle
58. Eases hot summer day sunburn
59. Explosive hit
61. Team AKA
62. Major head injury result
65. Twins AA team locale, state (short)
66. Western Baseball League

PUZZLE 7

	1	2	3	4		5	6	7	8		9	10	11	12
13						14					15			
16						17					18			
19						20				21				
22				23				24	25					
			26			27	28		29			30	31	32
33	34	35		36				37			38			
39			40		41				42					
43				44				45			46			
47			48			49				50				
			51		52			53			54	55	56	
57	58	59			60	61	62			63				
64				65				66						
67				68				69						
70				71				72						

Baseball Fact: "Take Me Out to the Ballgame", traditionally sung in the middle of the 7th inning is the unofficial anthem of American Baseball.

17

Across

1. Parking stub goes here
5. 50-50 ticket win, pay out
9. Helmet extension protects it
12. A's Outfielder #20 Mark
13. American Baseball Coaches Assoc.
14. Lower Mainland Baseball Assoc.
16. Baseball's "Big Papi"
17. Fast Fielder body type
18. Bat make-up
19. A league standard
20. Stadiums are built on
22. Players ___ to have attractive wives
23. Jays, Orioles or Cardinals mascot
24. Anthem instills it in fans
27. Twins most saves: 47 (2009)
29. A fastball AKA
31. MLB···. An "Organization", short
32. MLB owners shut things down, 1973 & 76
33. 2010 NL Gold Glove 3rd Base
36. Many leagues, many "classes" of play
37. Long-time announcer Vince Scully did it in 2016
39. Thrown ball at high-speed. Think green pod
40. "Extreme" ball altering took place pre 1920
41. Rangers Pitcher #39 Kolby
45. White Sox St. Pitcher #84 Dylan
46. Players are to a team wheel
48. Ticket $ales produce (slang)
50. Dodgers SS great Pokey or Pee Wee
52. MLB HQ, Avenue ___ Americas
53. The Yankees 27 WS wins is ___ in scale
56. MLB balls are hand-sewn in Costa ___
57. Alma ___, college ball
58. Rangers Pitcher #36 Hyeon Jong
59. 14x All-Star, 13x GG, "Pudge" Rodriguez
60. Stadium AKA
61. Times On Base, stat
62. League approved (short)
63. Tigers Pitcher #51 Garcia

Down

1. Yankees Pitcher #56 O'Day
2. Nationals Infielder #45 Yasel
3. 2019 NL Manager of the Year
4. Hit by pitch, player's mindset
5. Coach reaching-out to bullpen
6. Minnesota Twins Mascot
7. Steroid use in the 90's
8. Inside mitt
9. HOF J.L. Wilkinson
10. A Jumbotron
11. World Baseball Outreach
12. Cold weather dugout attire
15. Cubs St. Pitcher #73 Alzolay
21. "Exclusive" tickets
23. Red Sox Closer #19 Matt
25. MLB and owners ___ $ in, like leaves
26. Pro baller is a "God" to fans
28. Cubs Infielder #2 Nico
30. On the road player housings
33. Indians Catcher #46 Rivera
34. Red Sox Pitcher #0 Adam
35. Sports reporter, often accused of creating
37. A's most stolen bases, Henderson: 867
38. Pitcher, a fake motion to 1st is to what?
39. Parade AKA
42. Marlins Catcher #38 Jorge
43. Describes a team with a winless record
44. Pirates Pitcher w best W-L pct.: .731
47. Indians Outfielder #35 Mercado
49. True Earned Run Average
51. Brewers Pitcher #57 Yardley
52. Brewers Catcher #10 Narváez
54. Orioles Infielder #11 Valaika
55. Cottage Grove Baseball

PUZZLE 8

Baseball Fact: The average life span of a major league baseball is 5–7 pitches. During a typical game, an estimated 70+ balls are used.

Across

1. True Earned Run Average
5. Minnesota Twins Mascot
11. Pirates Infielders #38 Will
12. Yankees Infielder #18 Odor
14. Trade rumors need one
15. "Take me out to the ___"
16. Irate coach can be, from game, by Umpire
17. Yankees "Empire" NN
18. Houston on the scoreboard
19. Back up position player (short)
20. Injuries cause it
21. Draft "pickups" (slang)
22. Ticket price add-ons
24. Washington Nationals NN
25. Cleveland Indians Great Lake
26. Player's low cost agency
27. Company messages in stadium (short)
28. Pirates Pitcher w most shutouts: 44
29. Practice drills, over and over (short)
31. A teammate becomes one
32. MTV show, may have ballers home, cars
34. Catch AKA
35. Games time estimations: Abbr
39. Blooper collection on TV
40. 3x All-Star, 1x WS, 2001 NL saves leader relief pitcher ___ Nen
41. Pro baller bobble head
42. Add to a team's negative column
43. Straights of a $$$ struggling league
44. Run batted in
45. WS time (short)
46. The fan mail was ___ through USPS
47. R, is Runs ___
50. Must be when assessing draftees potential
52. Team loss, by a lot. Also, "extreme" injury
53. Beer guy offers a great one
54. Rays Pitcher #45 Honeywell
55. Ticket seller. Also, PBP guy
56. Beer holders. Also, trash holders

Down

1. Players agents, for investments
2. Holes for what? in batter's helmet
3. Twins most singles: 182 (1925)
4. Old stadiums like OAK's haven't done it well
5. Orioles Pitcher #70 Lakins
6. Pirates Outfielder #19 Moran
7. AAA Durham player (Rays affiliate)
8. A zero on the scoreboard (slang)
9. Angels City
10. Camera controls. Also, TV watchers clickers
11. Where tailgaters get their beer
13. Pro baller is a "God" to fans
14. Team support system
15. Loss hurt, "The team was given the ___" (slang)
20. San Diego Padres NN
21. Trading card "rated", like school
23. Sony's "MLB The Show" video games, years of
24. CLE Indians, known as the what in 1903-14?
25. 2x NL batting champ & Hall-of-Famer, Roush
28. Aurora University BaseBall
30. Elite Baseball League
31. Ruth
32. White Sox Pitcher #45 Garrett
33. Umps may oust players to ___ on-field order
34. White Sox AAA state ___ Carolina
36. Mariners Catcher #22 Luis
37. Mets Outfielder #4 Almora
38. Avoid the tag action
40. Wears his WS prize (slang)
42. Amount of beers drank at any game
43. Curveball AKA
46. Under the playing field
47. South Shore Baseball Club
48. Component ERA
49. Hot indoor stadium (slang)
51. Rancocas Valley semi-pro baseball League

PUZZLE 9

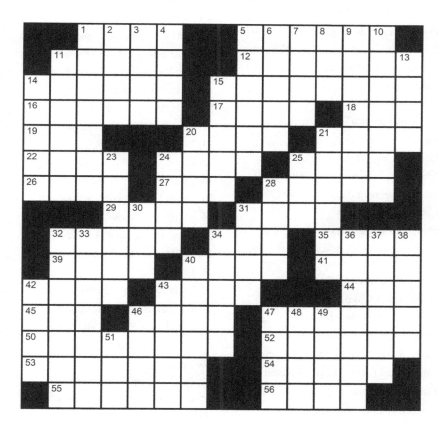

Baseball Fact: On April 14, 1910, William Taft (a former semipro BB player) became the 1st President to throw out an Opening Day game pitch. Except Jimmy Carter, Presidents have been tossing out Opening Day pitches ever since.

Across

1. Orioles most doubles: 56 (2009)
7. Brewers Catcher #9 Manny
11. Baltimore on the scoreboard
12. Ticket Sales produce (slang)
13. USA Baseball
14. Contract starter
17. Red Sox Pitcher #79 Bryan
18. Astros Infielder #84 Freudis
19. Player tryout. Also, a free sample (short)
20. Pitch ball over edge of HP, ___ the corner
22. Pitcher and batter's back-n-forth
23. Catch AKA
24. Rays Pitcher #21 Reed
25. MLB, live on YouTube
28. Fan admiration action
31. Base path trip AKA a dirt ___
32. Morganna, Kissing Bandit, other Bball
33. Summer game in ARZ, hot as this place
34. Concession beer rule
35. Players feeling about attending presser
38. League has enough funding. Also, horse house
40. Some stadium security's day job
41. White Sox AA locale, state (short)
43. Travel team's flight info: Abbr
44. Home Plate caller (short)
45. Home of Nevada's minor-league Aces
46. Composite of proposed new stadium
50. Game is broadcast on (short)
52. Anaheim Angels on scoreboard
54. Scored nothing
55. Bartman, famous interfering Cub fan
57. White Sox Infielder #1 Madrigal
59. Remove from stats calculation
60. MLB ___ ing Day, early April
61. 3rd jersey AKA
63. Affects hit ball's flight
64. Rangers, from the ___ star state

65. Losing teams pray to him
66. Keeps balls from entering stands. e.g Backstop
67. Made up of players

Down

1. No tickets left to buy
2. Rangers best batting avg: .319
3. Rangers Outfielder #41 White
4. City to city connection
5. Eight ___ dozen balls used in a typical game
6. Pitcher Bartolo Colon's biggest feature
7. "Get" ketchup from big bottle at concession
8. Orioles Pitcher #60 Mattson
9. Baseball and pastime
10. Trainers apply it to an injury
11. Wins bring fans "together"
15. Players AKA
16. Twins Pitcher #57 Hansel
21. Sportswriters "write" action
26. Minnesota Twins Mascot
27. Brewers Catcher #12 Luke
29. Ball grease to ball's flight
30. Home
35. Where a player is from
36. Baseball is as American as this baked good
37. Angels best SO to Walk: 2.92
39. Orioles Infielder #39 Rylan
40. Roster trims
42. Orioles most sac flies: 17 (1996)
47. Lowers value of old BB card
48. Sports writer's boss
49. Skills are tracked, formulated, judged
51. A ball game is a type of what?
53. Option for opening pitch, especially in L.A.
56. Game, when the 9th is done
58. Numbers game that sports betters like
62. Season tix, holds that seat (short)

PUZZLE 10

 (crossword grid)

Baseball Fact: Many visiting teams wear gray uniforms to differ from the home team. This dates back to the late 1800s when travelling teams lacked time to clean their uniforms so wore gray to hide dirt.

Across

1. Continental Amateur Baseball Assoc.
5. Alexandria Area Baseball Assoc.
9. Luxury box food offering
14. Abandon the previously agreed on call, or pitch
15. Nationals Infielder #7 Turner
16. Single-A baseball AKA
17. Twins most strikeouts: 178 (2016)
18. True Earned Run Average
19. Yankees Pitcher #85 Luis
20. Bottom of standings place (slang)
22. "Last place" position in the standings
23. Angels City
25. Indians Outfielder #40 Ramírez
29. Fans camera lights at night game
34. "A part" in a baseball movie
35. Umpire decision
37. VIP threw ceremonial 1st pitch, 1910
38. Astros Infielder #10 Gurriel
39. Astros Pitcher #67 Jairo
40. Players do not take PEDs, is a what?
41. Accesses the upper deck (short)
42. Highlight Of The Night - Sports Center
43. A's P w best win–loss pct: .712
44. Option for a Nationals game opening pitch thrower
46. Not as many runs as opponent
47. Indians Outfielder #1 Amed
50. A steroid user is labeled as one
54. Does not play Sony's MLB The Show, VG
59. League owners, and meeting room
60. White Sox Pitcher #65 Heuer
61. Team's super mascot wears one
62. Indians Infielder #84 Clement
63. Trade rumors, often ___ ymous
64. East Toronto Baseball Assoc.
65. A's career most doubles: 365
66. Braves career most stolen bases: 434
67. Tailgating BBQ cooking process

Down

1. College Baseball Scouting Bureau
2. Player's skill btw AAA and the majors
3. Stadium waste holders
4. Eases hot summer day sunburn
5. At live game
6. Stadium AKA
7. Gain playoff spot
8. Triple A ball
9. Mariners AAA team locale, WA
10. Gamblers make one on a game
11. Yesterday's game, happened in the
12. Shea stadium, 1974-75 home to Mets & ___ Yanks
13. Grand HR
21. Pro baseball participants
22. Used to buy tickets, non-credit
24. Phillies St. Pitcher #56 Zach
25. Wesley Snipes 1989 "Major League" movie character Willie Mays ___
26. A league standard
27. 2010 NL Gold Glove, 3rd Base
28. Twins most extra base hits: 84 (1964)
30. Trading card rating system
31. Los Angeles Angels NN
32. Error made by the third baseman
33. Team's bus driver, action
35. Colorado Rockies stadium, beer
36. Back up position player (short)
39. Team photo activity
43. Team's area fan base (short)
45. Personnel exchanges
46. Player pockets sticking out, shows what?
48. Pitcher's feat (slang) (3wd)
49. White Sox St. Pitcher #55 Carlos
50. Needed after long, tiring game
51. Cubs Pitcher #80 Abbott
52. Top Aaron of baseball
53. Cleveland Indians Great Lake
55. Standouts on the pitcher's mound
56. Half a teammate
57. Eden Prairie Baseball Assoc.
58. Planted in a stadium seat
60. 5 MLB team state (short)

PUZZLE 11

1	2	3	4		5	6	7	8		9	10	11	12	13
14					15					16				
17					18					19				
20				21				22						
			23				24							
25	26	27	28				29			30	31	32	33
34					35	36				37				
38				39					40					
41				42				43						
44				45				46						
			47			48	49							
50	51	52	53			54				55	56	57	58
59					60				61					
62				63				64						
65				66				67						

Baseball Fact: Fans eat 22+M hot dogs and 5.5M sausages during a major league season. That is enough hot dogs to stretch from L.A.'s Dodger Stadium to Chicago's Wrigley Field.

Across

1. Big Lake Baseball Assoc.
5. Asst. Coach to Head Coach
11. 2009 AL MVP
12. A fastball AKA
14. Catcher's glove is for a Pitcher
15. Bench warmer's jersey condition
16. E
17. Batter's helmet holes expose these
18. Computer Graphic Imagery, e.g. TV HUD
19. Avg of major leaguer is 29
20. 1st, 2nd, or 3rd
21. Knees and elbows, from turf contact
22. Orioles highest batting avg: .340 (2004)
24. Catcher's mask metal
25. Concession burger type
26. Best of the team or league
27. "Entire" roster list
28. 50-50 tix, a type of
29. Team's front office: Abbr
31. Fielder contacted ball with foot, error
32. Houston Astros NN
34. Minor Leaguers travel in it
35. Fried concession food ingredient
39. Bad team, descriptor
40. Top of stadium beer
41. Cleveland Indians Great Lake
42. Served at sports bar
43. Being a pro baller, many pros & few
44. Relief Failures, Pitcher stat
45. Contract agreement
46. Netherlands born, 20 season Fr. Twins Pitcher, Blyleven
47. Pitch result, good for thrower
50. Players on vacations, from baseball
52. Mets career best ERA: 2.57, Tom
53. Movement on a balk
54. Braves Manager #43 Snitker
55. Stadium capacity, counts this
56. Ump "decision"

Down

1. Nationals Catcher #38 Tres
2. Mets Pitcher #67 Seth
3. Alcoholic bevy at concession
4. Creative degree type of many college players
5. Press will to all, regarding a player scandal
6. Braves Infielder #23 Adrianza
7. Losers score vs winner
8. Orioles Infielder #11 Valaika
9. Admission to game bought online
10. Angels Infielder #2 Luis
11. Rays Outfielder #13 Manuel
13. A champion's time, ruling over team-league
14. Thirty in MLB
15. Braves AA team locale, Mississippi
20. Orioles city (short)
21. MLB will do this to avoid the courts
23. On-field coach's signal to batter
24. Many Alabama AAA, AA teams, nicknames
25. Noise from an unhappy fan
28. Add to a team's negative column
30. Losing teams pray to him
31. Clydesdale-horse ads, beer brand (short)
32. Distraction plays
33. Players agents, for investments
34. Drag, squeeze, sacrifice
36. Team when they land in visitor city
37. Orioles most GIDP: 32 (1985)
38. Coaches to asst. coaches
40. Stat columns "organized"
42. Stadium Greek food choice
43. White Sox St. Pitcher #84 Dylan
46. Baseball Editorials Analysis & Talk. Also, a policeman's area of patrol
47. South Shore Baseball Club
48. True Earned Run Average
49. Early MLB baseballers travelled by
51. Richmond Baseball Academy

PUZZLE 12

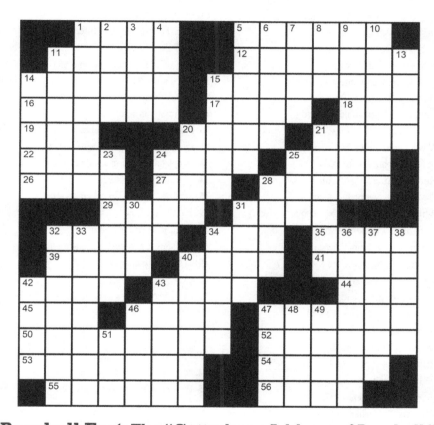

Baseball Fact: The "Gettysburg Address of Baseball." In 1939 after 17 seasons, 36-year-old Lou Gehrig retired because of amyotrophic lateral sclerosis (ALS). He said in his farewell speech he was "the luckiest man on the face of the earth."

Across

1. Red Sox Pitcher #79 Bryan
5. "We tried but ___ , we lost"
9. Struggling pitcher does to all bases
14. Opening Day, begin "fresh"
15. Players give away tickets to friends
16. Free ticket, an ___ Oakley
17. Take a base quickly for a score
19. A celeb's opening pitch distance, usually
20. Orioles most walks: 118 (1975)
21. First extra inning
22. Morganna, Kissing Bandit, other Bball
23. True Earned Run Average
25. Ret. players feel it, and want to return
29. Brewer St. Pitcher #39 Burnes
33. Condition of low value BB card
34. Tigers Catcher #13 Haase
36. Washington, for the Mariners
37. Braves city on a scoreboard
38. Phillies Outfielder #24 Quinn
40. Playing card complete collection
41. White Sox best ERA, 1.81 (also MLB Rec.)
44. Light hit description. Also a finger action
45. Eye protection, name (slang)
46. Brewers Pitcher w the most wins: 117
48. Well-known baseball research, Saber___
50. Ret. players get it, and want to return
52. Nationals city on a scoreboard
53. Walk Rate, stat
56. Pads help with the shock ___
62. BB appeals to young and old fans ___
63. Bad player criticism, nasty shout (3wd)
64. Heard during batters intros
65. Mariners St. Pitcher #50 Swanson
66. New Lowell Minor Baseball
67. A try-hard player is said to have this
68. Groups of plays
69. Dallas Amateur Baseball Assoc.

Down

1. Run type of baseball cards
2. MLB has been accused of ___ trust
3. Too old for Little League
4. Most Valuable baseball card
5. Steroid user label
6. Money from big contract (slang)
7. Negotiation benefit (slang)
8. A term meaning "tired" from the game
9. Houston Astros NN
10. Where fans place their hand during anthem
11. Trade rumors, often ___ ymous
12. Surrounds the infield
13. Mets Pitcher #67 Lugo
18. Little League Baseball International
24. HOF Earle Combs
25. Sum of all stats attempts into one
26. Fan scream (slang)
27. Roster "trim", off the top
28. Common fan sign
30. Practice hones this level of skills
31. Listed on concession board
32. Keeps balls from entering stands. e.g Backstop
33. Detroit Tigers Mascot
35. Stadium concession baked good
39. TV Broadcasters
42. Team logo on fan's bumper
43. "___ ticket in town", for on-fire team
45. Team break-apart
47. HOF Nestor Chylak
49. Likely-hood of a small-market team winning multiple WS
51. Wesley Snipes 1989 "Major League" movie character Willie Mays ___
53. Play hard players take it w ice, post game
54. A core color of KC Royals brand
55. Brewers Catcher #9 Manny
57. Uneventful game, descriptor
58. Pre-game player attire that MLB likes
59. International Baseball League of Australia
60. Toes during snowy April opener
61. Georgina Minor Baseball Assoc.

PUZZLE 13

1	2	3	4		5	6	7	8		9	10	11	12	13
14					15					16				
17				18						19				
20										21				
		22						23	24					
	25	26				27	28		29			30	31	32
33					34			35		36				
37					38				39			40		
41			42	43		44					45			
46					47		48			49				
		50			51			52						
53	54	55				56	57	58				59	60	61
62					63									
64					65					66				
67					68					69				

Baseball Fact: On June 1963 Mets eccentric player Jimmy Piersall celebrated his 100th home run by running the bases backwards. He also inspired the 1955 memoir and 1957 movie Fear Strikes Out.

Across

1. Speech after pitch to the head
5. High velocity fastball
9. How often the Yankees win the WS
13. Error made by the pitcher
14. Gain playoff spot
15. Pro baller is a "God" to fans
16. Pitch slang - down ___ street, over the plate
17. "Angry" baseball player from bad call
18. Catcher's face protection
19. "Heavy" ball altering took place pre 1920
21. A
23. Rangers Pitcher #47 Hunter
24. When a batter swings at ball outside SZ
25. National Baseball Day
28. Braves most complete games: 476
30. Lights during night games
32. Pitcher Maglie "The Barber" of the 1950s Giants
33. Pros off-season gain
37. Players try to quit, still chewing tobacco
39. Astros Pitcher #67 Jairo
40. Blue Jays most games played by P, 505
42. Toledo Baseball Organization
45. Scored "nothing"
46. Indians Pitcher #37 Trevor
48. Defensive Efficiency Rating
49. Twins Pitcher #66 Jorge
51. Tailgate BBQ rack of
54. Bat diameter, ___ at handle end
55. Coaches "draw up" new plays
59. Stats
60. Minor League RubberDucks, Ohio
62. Team memo, subject line: Abbr
63. All-Star break days
64. MLB chew and spit sunflower food
65. Rich, buff player
66. Popular MLB sponsor type, vroom-vroom
67. Star player may live on it, fall off of it
68. Fan crowds. Also, organized criminals

Down

1. A lesser pro
2. A team's support from a bank
3. Team AKA. Also, a team within a team
4. A contract come-again
5. Braves Outfielder #38 Guillermo
6. Pitcher stat that's better when it's lower
7. Done w a C-flap, to a helmet
8. Major Leagues AKA
9. Fans need to enter ballpark
10. Field time agreement
11. Ump kicks-out coach
12. Calm fan disapproval
14. Blue Jays AAA team name
20. Number, short
22. Ticket numbers $old
25. National Baseball Hall of Fame
26. Minnesota Twins Mascot
27. Dallas Amateur Baseball Assoc.
29. Uniform's made of it
31. Done to schooling for Opening Day
34. Fans after a win. Also, garbage bag brand
35. BB gloves are made from it
36. MLB Comish AKA (slang)
38. Put together scores
41. Team does for unneeded player
43. Scannable on tickets
44. Concession hot-dog bitter topping
47. Your car during the game
49. Cubs Catcher #75 Miguel
50. Games to be played, not now but…
52. HOF Bill McGowan
53. Gatorade electrolytes prevent muscle ___
54. Southern Districts Baseball Club
56. Blue Jays Infielders #72 López
57. Ticket remainder
58. Game, when the 9th is done
61. MLB games, 9 innings (short)

PUZZLE 14

Baseball Fact: From a 90-mph pitch, a connected ball leaves the bat at a speed of 110 mph.

Across

1. Beach Collegiate Baseball League
5. Atlantic League of Prof. Baseball
9. Much of the back of a baseball card
14. Angels AA team, state (short)
15. Concession option
16. A try-hard player is said to have this
17. Under the playing field's grass
18. Mariners Infielder #12 White
19. All American Amateur Baseball Assoc.
20. Interference, stat
21. Watch the game while eating here
23. Yankees Pitcher #85 Luis
26. Reds AA team locale, state (short)
27. A's Outfielder #13 Luis
30. Complete Game Losses
33. Time of game - 7th in. stretch (est.)
35. Cleat
36. Angels most at bats per strikeout: 14.7
37. MLB cheating check
39. Diamond Backs territory (short)
40. Trying to win, have not
41. A weekend game day (short)
42. Indians DH #32 Reyes
44. "#1" finger
45. San Diego Padres stadium
49. Pitcher nods ups-down for a sign
55. Astros/Colt .45s on a scoreboard
56. Baseball (short)
57. HOF Rickey Henderson when stealing
58. Stadium beer toppers
59. MLB says no to this bat material
60. Stadium beer option
61. Fr. 2B, 3x All-star ___ Boone
62. Stadium maintenance teams
63. Baserunning challenge level after hitting HR
64. More players to rosters

Down

1. Old stadium bench seating, nothing fancy
2. Coach's wish they could "make more", of star player
3. Trade rumors for press to eat up
4. Longmont Baseball League
5. Pitcher who kept them off the scoreboard
6. Fans adoring emotion for a winner
7. Many modern stadium's façade, material
8. Term for a dugout heckling the Pitcher
9. Twins Pitcher #41 Anderson
10. Ticket taker action
11. Player's skill btw AAA and the majors
12. Tacoma Rainiers Baseball Network
13. Info about a player's career (short)
22. Angels City
24. Rangers Pitcher #66 Josh
25. Fans relief
28. Fans "root, root ___ the home team"
29. Score AKA
30. High and Inside pitch, music
31. Show, by an awful team. Also, 70s game show
32. Groin injury is actually this body part
33. True Earned Run Average
34. 2nd stringers do it for an opportunity
35. Attendance turn counter
36. Public Address System
37. Sunny day at the ballpark perk
38. Wet field error
40. Mets Pitcher #27 Jeurys
43. Presser response goes on and on
44. 2nd string ___ in for injured players
46. Rarely worn jersey type
47. Tickets bar lines
48. Umpire kicks-out coach
49. China Baseball Marketing Corp
50. Twins Pitcher #82 Bailey
51. Blue Jays Pitcher #24 Pearson
52. Bad strategy has at least one
53. Salty concession snack
54. Yanks road uniform, when in Canada
58. Lakeville Baseball Assoc.

PUZZLE 15

1	2	3	4		5	6	7	8		9	10	11	12	13
14					15					16			
17					18					19			
20					21			22					
23			24	25			26						
			27		28	29					30	31	32
	33	34							35			
36						37		38				
39					40							
41				42	43							
			44					45		46	47	48
49	50	51	52			53	54			55		
56				57				58				
59				60				61				
62				63				64				

Baseball Fact: The first pro game aired on television was a doubleheader between Brooklyn and Cincinnati on August 26, 1939.

33

Across

1. Grand Slams: Abbr
5. Austin Metro Baseball League
9. Old time word for bat
14. Actor Charlie Sheen as Ricky "Wild Thing" Vaughn in Major League movie
15. Strike - down the ___ , over the plate
16. Attendance turn counter
17. Error made by the shortstop
18. Coach's "strategy"
19. Wesley Snipes 1989 "Major League" movie character Willie Mays ___
20. Blue Jays Infielders #5 Santiago
22. A game loss, within the standings
24. When a plate crossing has not happened
25. Hole type in batter's helmet
26. Game is at its "end"
27. Yankees manager won 7 WS (latest 1958)
32. WS game 7, of games
34. Ticket number-bar
35. Coach encouragement, talk
36. Sacrifice, stat
37. They fill the stands
41. Concession food, comes w marinara sauce
44. Stadium location
46. NE state cheers for Red Sox as well (short)
47. Texas Baseball Club
48. Choke ___ = losses done beautifully well
52. Best of the pros. Also, a mid-season game
56. Indians Pitcher #37 Trevor
57. A mark made on telestrator
58. Reds Pitcher #50 Garrett
60. Early N.Y. Giants field, ___ Grounds
61. Minnesota Twins Mascot
62. Brewers Catcher #9 Manny
63. Records are for the best ___
64. Anthem leader does it
65. Coaches demeanor during the big game
66. Done for P.E.D.s

Down

1. Yankees Pitcher #57 Chad
2. Phillies Pitcher #60 Ramón
3. Pitcher moves, may cause balk
4. Baseball terms, slang
5. MLB's top licensed money maker
6. Cubs Pitcher #72 Tyson
7. Baseball Players Assoc.
8. Players vision correction tool
9. Bats are made from
10. Team trying something, maybe sharp
11. Player to fan greeting
12. Night games need this power (short)
13. Sportscaster sits at one
21. Astros Infielder #84 Freudis
23. Concession offering
28. HOF Nolan Ryan
29. Partial understanding of a rule
30. Player's skill btw AAA and the majors
31. Many leagues file this way
32. Term for fielders throwing to each other carefully, e.g. 1B to P
33. An Apple brand game streaming device
35. Pitches Per Plate Appearance
38. HOF Phil Rizzuto
39. Yankees "NY"
40. East Side Baseball Assoc.
41. Actor does of player, for a BB film
42. Contract upping
43. Bit of sports page article
45. Minor league players barely ___ by ($)
46. Trading card preservation
49. Action may start a bench brawl
50. ESPN documentary telling
51. Live dog mascot nose noise
52. Oakland Athletics NN
53. Little League Baseball International
54. By not making stadium payments
55. "Catch" ball, sometimes w great effort
59. MLB HQ, ___ town Manhattan

PUZZLE 16

1	2	3	4		5	6	7	8		9	10	11	12	13
14					15					16				
17					18					19				
20				21			22	23						
24							25							
			26				27			28	29	30	31	
	32	33						34						
35											36			
37			38	39	40			41	42	43				
44					45		46							
			47				48				49	50	51	
52	53	54	55				56							
57					58	59				60				
61					62					63				
64					65					66				

Baseball Fact: The franchise with the most players in the Hall of Fame is the San Francisco Giants (Fr. N.Y. 1883-1957), with 24.

Across

1. Baseball, the national ___ime
5. 1909 AL Batting Triple Crown
9. "Catch" ball, sometimes w great effort
13. 2013 NLCS MVP
14. Mood of struggling players (short)
15. Baseball cork location
16. Station condition when reporting game
17. Fans after a win. Also, garbage bag brand
18. Highlight Of The Night - Sports Center
19. MLB TV partner in Canada. Also, dings
20. Pirates colors resemble what insect?
21. Padding in a helmet
22. A double header lasts
24. Rich, buff player
26. Online posting method of scores, news
29. Exchanges money for tickets
33. Team's bus needs it, to go
36. Team's do to skills of new players
38. Pro ballers clubhouse (slang)
39. Hard hit grounder AKA a ___ Cutter
41. Non playoff team efforts, said to be
42. Marlins Infielder #5 Jon
43. Big Bad Baseball Annual
44. Bet on the game
46. Baseman: Abbr
47. Phones into a sports radio show
49. Orioles Pitcher #66 Tanner
51. Alaska Youth Baseball League
53. Old balls are ___ for batting practice
57. Hit batter gives the fans quite the ___
60. Seattle is ___ team, most years
63. Heckling is to "provoke" a Pitcher
64. 5 MLB team state (short)
65. AAA Durham player (Rays affiliate)
66. "Cy" Award named for the winningest pitcher of all time
67. Eases hot summer day sunburn
68. Team rivalry. Also Steve Harvey Family show
69. Angels St. Pitcher #37 Dylan
70. Baltimore's: Abbr
71. Team's top exec (short)
72. League corporate structure: Abbr

Down

1. MLB execs deciding rules sit on it
2. Base Umpire makes it on a play
3. 2019 NL Manager of the Year
4. Grip improving substance, Pine ___
5. Live mascot home
6. Fans "stare" at pro players
7. Top execs in the MLB. Also, instrument type
8. Boston Doves (1907–1910): Abbr
9. Team play time, date listing
10. Game start time in EST is 3pm, PST?
11. Electronic ___ maker of fr. MLB Triple Play video game series
12. Griffey Sr. passed the BB one to Griffey Jr.
13. Weighted On Base Average
20. All-Star break days
21. Dynamic two-some e.g. work-well together
23. Their field
25. MLB Network partner
27. East Side Baseball Assoc.
28. Thirty in MLB
30. Uniform is a type of
31. H
32. Grass crew will, pre-game
33. Go Deep Baseball Camps
34. All American Baseball Assoc.
35. Sylmar Independent Baseball League
37. Southern Districts Baseball Club
40. Dumping players decreases what?
42. Vegas takes, on all leagues
44. Greg Reinhard Baseball
45. Crowd level after a score
48. Diff. "level" type pitches, to lead the batter
50. How a rundown usually ends
52. Brewers Pitcher #52 Eric
54. Signature = player is, to his MLB contract
55. Stadiums are built on open, or cleared ones
56. Coaches demeanor during the big game
57. Turf burn heal mark
58. Umpire decision
59. How often the Yankees win the WS
61. Jays
62. American League Division Series
65. Batters Facing Pitcher
66. Youth Baseball League

PUZZLE 17

Baseball Fact: Chicago's Wrigley Field was the last MLB park to install lights. Until 1988, the Cubs played all their home games during the day.

Across

1. Southside Pony Baseball League
5. On a rope in the player's locker room
9. Germantown Baseball League
12. Hit batter, gives the fans quite the ___
13. MLB hedging, insur ___
14. Most baseball career lengths
16. Eight ___ dozen balls used in a typical game
17. Player must dress, pre game arrival
18. Every team's is to win the World Series
19. Indians Infielders #71 Gabriel
20. Unlike NFL, MLB games are not on one
22. 2016 WS MVP Zobrist & Twin CF #11 Revere
23. Team ownership change, result of a
24. Long presser response (slang)
27. Describes a team with a sour, bad record
29. Swap a player for another
31. Like some batteries & baseball leagues
32. Made it to The Bigs, or "I have ___ "
33. Error, ball falls out of fielders gloves
36. College ballers may be on paid/free ___
37. Signal from a pitcher to Catcher
39. Cubs Pitcher #43 Winkler
40. AL & NL in 2000, merged ___ MLB org
41. "Draw" fans in to watch the game
45. Press does w player controversies, like a chef does with soup
46. Off season workout w weights
48. Astros Outfielder #220 McCormick
50. Braves Infielder #23 Adrianza
52. Teams on west and east
53. Error made by the pitcher
56. 14x All-Star, 13x GG, "Pudge" Rodriguez
57. Free ticket, an ___ Oakley
58. HR - ___ long distance, saying
59. Keeps balls from entering stands. e.g Backstop
60. Pitcher's arm muscle, common injury
61. Little League Baseball
62. Cleared from a game field, pre-construction
63. Pitcher who kept them off the scoreboard

Down

1. One who scores
2. Rays Pitcher #61 Luis
3. Off center logo area on many jerseys
4. Cinematic game capture (camera)
5. 2006 AL Pitching Triple Crown
6. Pirates Infielders #61 Cruz
7. Captures the game
8. Mets Infielder #20 Alonso
9. Garciaparra Baseball Group
10. Allow tying run to score
11. Collectables and memorabi ___
12. Team trying something, maybe sharp
15. Game is finished
21. 2nd run of trading card
23. BB has a regular and pre
25. Dirtied a uniform, baserunner action
26. Standouts on the pitcher's mound
28. On-field coach hand-to-face signal
30. Foul or "stray" ball
33. Umpire will change a ball w this damage
34. Calm response to presser Q&A
35. Yankees Infielder #18 Rougned
37. The fans, loudly at bad team (snake)
38. Term describes "To pitch". Also, FedEx duty
39. Fielded players
42. Term describing a long-time baseball star
43. Orioles Catcher #15 Sisco
44. To score w men on base vs none
47. Mood of player called out from very bad call
49. Stadium climber
51. Draftees ___ at what team they want to play for
52. Continental Amateur Baseball Assoc.
54. Rub for glove
55. Euro League Baseball

PUZZLE 18

Baseball Fact: Today 100+ countries make up the International Baseball Federation. Japan's Nippon league is the largest pro baseball league outside the U.S.

Across

1. Hitter type w a high average, but low power
5. Airmail - throw error, may land here
11. Brewers Catcher #12 Luke
12. Rangers Outfielder #3 Leody
14. Nationals Pitcher #21 Rainey
15. Dangle $ in front of players, does what?
16. Batting second
17. New team's franchise fee, to be paid
18. Something credited to a pitcher
19. Montreal Expos, as was seen on scoreboards
20. Betting terminology
21. 9th of a game's innings, unless tied
22. How often the Yankees win the WS
24. Grass crews equipment storage place
25. Artificial playing surface
26. A's Outfielder #15 Brown
27. Young baseball fan
28. Mets Pitcher #29 Hunter
29. Shea stadium, 1974-75 home to Mets & ___ Yanks
31. Bay Area Texas Baseball
32. Jerseys letters, held on with ___ es
34. Light tag
35. East Side Baseball Assoc.
39. Throw AKA
40. Run type of most baseball cards
41. Natural grass
42. Pitchers Feller, Lemon & Gibson
43. Needed for WS security, extra
44. Back up position player (short)
45. Inherited Runs Allowed, stat
46. Force that alters ball flight
47. MLB will do, to avoid the courts
50. Rays Pitcher #34 Trevor
52. First game of season
53. Pitcher will make a fake motion to 1st
54. HOF Rickey Henderson when stealing
55. Stat columns "organized"
56. MIA and TB foliage

Down

1. Place for a pickup game
2. Mark made on telestrator
3. Brewers Pitcher #50 Bettinger
4. MLB players flying first-class
5. Traveling team's bags, on plane
6. Home run (food, slang)
7. Loyal, regular fan
8. A's AAA team locale, state (short)
9. Pitcher motions arm back
10. Owners sign talent to ___ the fans
11. 1956 AL Batting Triple Crown, M.M.
13. Pitcher failed, was ___ off by coach
14. Mets Catcher #3 Nido
15. Montreal Expos___ to D.C., - Nationals
20. Indians state
21. Bat AKA
23. Angels Infielder #23 Matt
24. ScoreKeep ShortHand: Abbr
25. Totals (short)
28. Concession beer servers
30. League Championship Series
31. Marlins Pitcher #52 Anthony
32. Press articles
33. Chew
34. Old VCR recorded games are on them
36. Ticket seat info (2nd wd - short)
37. Baseball player, slang
38. Ball grease to ball flight
40. Helmets to head shape
42. Jays, Orioles or Cardinals mascot
43. Dispose of batter quickly
46. Players stride, walk & run
47. On a rope in the player's locker room
48. Eden Prairie Baseball Assoc.
49. Baserunner twitch, like poker signs
51. Not one in the MLB

PUZZLE 19

Baseball Fact: The most valuable trading card is the 1909 Honus Wagner T206 card, worth appx. $2.8 million.

Across

1. Morganna, Kissing Bandit
7. Brewers Catcher #9 Manny
11. Baltimore on the scoreboard
12. Ticket $ales produce (slang)
13. USA Baseball
14. Contract starter
17. Red Sox Pitcher #79 Bryan
18. Astros Infielder #84 Freudis
19. Player tryout. Also, a free sample (short)
20. Pitch ball over edge of HP, ___ the corner
22. Pitcher and batter's back-n-forth
23. Catch AKA
24. Pirates Pitcher #44 Ponce
25. Live MLB on YouTube
28. Fan admiration action
31. Base path trip AKA a dirt ___
32. Morganna, Kissing Bandit, other Bball
33. Summer game in ARZ, hot as this place
34. Concession beer rule
35. Players about attending presser
38. League has enough funding. Also, horse house
40. Some stadium security's day job
41. White Sox AA locale, state (short)
43. Game time estimation: Abbr
44. Umpire (short)
45. Home of Nevada's minor-league Aces
46. Composite of new stadium
50. Game is broadcast on (short)
52. Anaheim Angels on the scoreboard
54. Scored nothing
55. Angels Pitcher #40 Cishek
57. Wear on a trading card, decreases value
59. Remove from stats calculation
60. MLB ___ ing Day, early April
61. 3rd jersey AKA
63. Twins AA team name, ___ Surge
64. Fastball sign, finger(s)

65. Losing teams pray to him
66. Keeps balls from entering stands. e.g Backstop
67. Players make it up

Down

1. No tickets left to buy
2. Rangers best batting avg: .319
3. Indians Pitcher #78 Morgan
4. Yanks Gray uniform
5. Eight ___ dozen balls used in a typical game
6. Pitcher Bartolo Colon's biggest feature
7. Double "clutch"
8. Orioles Pitcher #60 Mattson
9. 1 of 2 leagues, MLB
10. Trainers apply it to an injury
11. Wins bring fans "together"
15. The players AKA
16. Twins Pitcher #57 Hansel
21. Press does this to describe the action, in the papers
26. Minnesota Twins Mascot
27. Brewers Catcher #12 Luke
29. Ball grease to ball flight
30. Home
35. Where a player is from
36. Baseball is as American as this baked good
37. Angels best SO to Walk: 2.92
39. Orioles Infielder #39 Rylan
40. Roster trims
42. Orioles most sac flies: 17 (1996)
47. Lowers value of old BB card
48. Sports writer's boss
49. Skills are tracked, formulated, assessed
51. Baseball game, an "affair" AKA
53. Option for opening pitch
56. Game, when the 9th is done
58. Numbers game sports betters like
62. Season tix, holds that seat (short)

PUZZLE 20

Baseball Fact: Minor and major league bats are made from wood. Metal-made bats are used at the college level.

Across

1. ScoreKeep ShortHand: Abbr
5. Process stats (short)
9. A's Pitcher #50 Mike F
14. Bell, that sponsors the All-Star Legends
15. Team's should, regarding league rules
16. Indians Infielder #84 Clement
17. Oakland Athletics NN
18. Weighted Runs Above Average
19. 18 season Pitcher, Mike Mussina w 270 wins, NN
20. Twins boast this # of AL batting champs
22. Blue Jays Catcher #9 Danny
23. ___ MLB collectables are more valuable than common items
25. Business mens interests in a league
29. Many pro leagues vs MLB
34. Lots of fouled-off pitches, does to pitcher
35. Package of 12 baseballs
37. A team's territory AKA
38. A champion's time, ruling over team-league
39. Ticket bar lines
40. Metal bat strike noise
41. Ump can "kick-out" coach
42. Team came up short
43. Field time agreement
44. Indians career most doubles, 486
46. Not as many runs as opponent
47. Washed-up player
50. 1995 Tiger OTY - .275 avg; 81 RBIs
54. Washed-up player (3wd)
59. Single-A baseball AKA
60. Pray to this Norse god for win
61. Wrong time swing, miss
62. Tigers Infielder #9 Castro
63. Mood of struggling player (short)
64. All Star Baseball Academy
65. Nova Scotia Senior Baseball League
66. Player is "happy" to sign
67. Holds uniform pants in place

Down

1. Cards batting great___ the Man Musial
2. Pirates Outfielder #60 Tom
3. Ticket checker light-gun action
4. Strong fire-man like throwing arm (slang)
5. Royals most games: 162 (1977)
6. Yankees Pitcher #84 Albert
7. Batter crowds plate
8. Cy Young Award
9. A lady baseball fan
10. Cal Ripken Jr. is this Man
11. Baseball HOFer "Slaughter", Bradsher
12. Win effect on rankings
13. Already watched game
21. Early week game day (short)
22. Pirates Outfielder #14 Oliva
24. Player mood after a loss
25. Houston Astros NN
26. Done with shoe lace
27. Trade discussions after bad game
28. Twins St. Pitcher #18 Maeda
30. Schedules are full of them
31. Indians Infielder #71 Gabriel
32. Stiff grip
33. A rookies pre game feeling
35. Colorado Rockies stadium, beer
36. Company messages in stadium (short)
39. Hit ball goes through infield, untouched
43. Players vision correction tool
45. Mets Outfielder #26 Lee
46. No talent teams ___ just a few players
48. Stadium security's star
49. Braves Infielder #23 Adrianza
50. Fans do this over pro ballers
51. RBI single
52. Kansas City Royals NN
53. McKinney Little League Baseball
55. Play by play'ers do it well
56. MLB teams can beat semi-pro teams with it
57. East Toronto Baseball League
58. Player must dress, pre game arrival
60. Athletics city on a scoreboard

PUZZLE 21

1	2	3	4		5	6	7	8		9	10	11	12	13
14					15					16				
17					18					19				
20				21					22					
			23				24							
25	26	27	28				29			30	31	32	33	
34					35	36				37				
38				39					40					
41				42				43						
44			45					46						
			47			48	49							
50	51	52	53			54			55	56	57	58		
59					60				61					
62				63				64						
65				66				67						

Baseball Fact: The batting helmet earflap became an MLB requirement in 1983. In related news, wearing hockey helmets were optional in the NHL before June 1979.

Across

1. 1-for-1 player trade
5. Mets most walk-off RBI: 10
11. Brewers Catcher #12 Luke
12. A drink size at concession
14. Nationals Pitcher #21 Rainey
15. HR - ___ for long distance
16. Batting second
17. Indians Catcher #46 Rivera
18. Game time estimation: Abbr
19. Fr. Montreal Expos on a scoreboard
20. 2016 WS MVP Zobrist & Twin CF #11 Revere
21. MLB Comish AKA (slang)
22. How often the Yankees win the WS
24. Seattle is ___ team, most years
25. Mariners Pitcher #43 Juan
26. Nationals Pitcher #56 Romero
27. Baseman: Abbr
28. 2013 NL Wilson Defensive POY
29. MLB balls are hand-sewn in Costa ___
31. Team's super mascot wears one
32. A player does this to gaps
34. Philadelphia Phillies: Abbr
35. Pitchers weapons
39. Add to a team's negative column
40. Pirates Outfielder #60 Tom
41. CAN has one ___ in MLB
42. Actors in a baseball movie
43. Injured player suffers with it
44. MLB teams travel ___ airplane
45. Used to watch a game
46. Messed up play, mild reaction
47. Player feelings after a WS win
50. Presser "reply"
52. Angels Closer #32 Iglesias
53. Just before majors
54. Game is over
55. Tactics to waste time. Also, horse homes
56. Old stadiums like OAK's haven't done it well

Down

1. Place for a pickup game
2. Sparkling kind, to celebrate WS win
3. Cubs Pitcher #30 Mills
4. MLB players getting to fly first-class
5. Pirates P w most losses: 218
6. Batter crowds plate
7. Fans "stare" at pro players
8. Player's action after connecting w the ball
9. Marlins Pitcher #57 Hernández
10. Royals Pitcher #54 Ervin
11. Where to keep a championship trophy
13. Planted in a stadium seat
14. Mets Catcher #3 Nido
15. "Imagine" a WS victory
20. Braidwood Baseball Softball Assoc.
21. New team within another team's territory
23. Base-stealer rockets off with a lot of it
24. Baseball broadcaster until 1990s, + s
25. Stadium Beer and soda comes from one
28. Big ___, David Ortiz NN
30. Innings Per Start, stat
31. 1st S. Korean in MLB ___ Ho Park, 1994-2010
32. No-coach team meeting, ___ only
33. A team that fails to score in a game does what?
34. Pitcher, Satchel in the HOF
36. Changed contract
37. The fan letter was ___ through USPS
38. S Jersey
40. Twins AA team state
42. League approved (short)
43. MLB execs deciding rules sit on one. Manual score "cards" on non electric board
46. Pro baller bobble head
47. Nationals Infielder #7 Turner
48. Term, to "place" score panel on scoreboard
49. Pro's hot new car (slang).
51. Pitches Per Plate Appearance

PUZZLE 22

Baseball Fact: 5 - 7 inches from the barrel end of a bat is known as the "sweet spot". Connecting here produces less vibration resulting in more HRs and that satisfying "crack" sound.

Across

1. Ontario Senior Baseball Assoc.
5. MLB Comish if ruling country
9. 2 cleats make 1
14. 1 finger ___ s fastball
15. Overspending leagues fall into a deep one
16. Field time agreement
17. Catcher equipment known as Tools of ___
19. American Amateur Athletic Baseball Assoc.
20. Healthy concession food, unfortunately
21. Score is all tied up, it's like a ___ new game
22. Team joker, oink-oink
23. Pitchers stats
25. New York Mets NN
29. A bat's finish descriptor
33. Condition of low value BB card
34. Players do them in the weight room
36. Free ticket, an ___ Oakley
37. Atlanta on the scoreboard
38. Players run out of it late in game
40. 90's was the homerun "time"
41. White Sox best ERA, 1.81 (also MLB Rec.)
44. Truck that transports team equipment
45. Athletes abandon it in the off-season
46. Brewers Pitcher w most wins: 117
48. Long BB article, very in-depth w the ___
50. Retired players get it, and want to return
52. Chicago White Sox: Abbr
53. Walk Rate, stat
56. Ball bounces 1x before fielder plays it
62. BB appeals to young and old fans ___
63. Alternative to sports on cable
64. Heard during batters intros
65. East Metro Baseball League
66. American Professional Baseball Assoc.
67. No-quit players have it
68. 2 contract yeses equal what?
69. Fan noise

Down

1. "Remove" from stats calculation
2. Sonic maker & Fr. maker of top MLB VG
3. MLB does to cheaters
4. Current Pitcher failed, time to call ___
5. Twins Pitcher #62 Dakota
6. Strike ___
7. AL Division Series winners meet in this
8. Blue Jays Catcher #7 McGuire
9. Rays AA team locale (state)
10. Angels most at bats per strikeout: 14.7
11. Player's skill btw AAA and the majors
12. This baseball book's legal ID: Abbr
13. Absorb the sports page
18. 50-50 ticket physical organization
24. HOF Ray Schalk
25. TC, ___ Chances
26. Fan voice, loud noise (slang)
27. Completed trading card ___ , bundles
28. Stealer needs it to succeed
30. Pirates Infielders #61 Cruz
31. Lots of fouled-off pitches, does to pitcher
32. Pitcher's throw it, hot
33. Detroit Tigers Mascot
35. Yanks and Mets city
39. 1989 NL MVP
42. Team logo on fan's bumper
43. Ticket in town, for on-fire team
45. Game info on TV screen - Heads Up ___
47. HOF Nestor Chylak
49. Miss practice, unexpectedly, without reason
51. Team or player, "shafted"
53. Players take it w ice, post game
54. Jays
55. Brewers Catcher #9 Manny
57. ID on jersey
58. East Toronto Baseball Assoc.
59. Strike - down the ___ , over plate
60. East Toronto Baseball League
61. Natural grass

PUZZLE 23

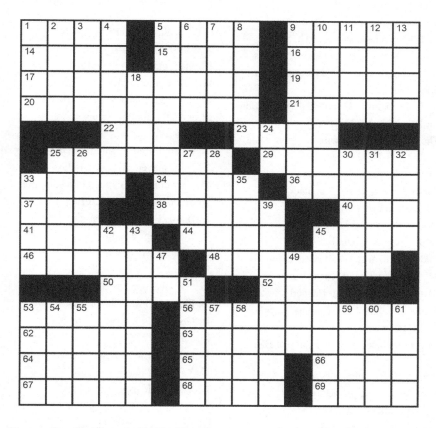

Baseball Fact: L.A. Dodgers, originally founded in Brooklyn N.Y., are named for the noted skill the residents displayed at "dodging" city trolleys.

Across

1. "Holes" created in the field
5. Process stats (short)
9. Nebraska American Legion Baseball
13. Team AKA. Also, a team within a team
14. Clemens was deemed one, regarding PEDs
15. A team's territory AKA
16. Nationals Manager 2007-09, Manny
17. DP between SS and 2B
18. Holds concession food in transit
19. Well-known baseball research, Saber___
21. A player's ___ speak louder than words
23. Cleared from a game field, construction
24. Tosses ball
25. MLB The Show VG mobile platform, Sony
28. Little leaguer age bracket
30. The Yankees 27 WS wins is ___ in scale
32. CAN MLB TV show'er
33. Ticket taker, does to tix
37. 2 outs, baserunners ___ contact
39. Concession pizza division
40. Orioles St. Pitcher #64 Dean
42. Little League Baseball
45. Slidell Bantam Baseball Association
46. MLB in the terms of league status
48. Mariners Outfielder #0 Haggerty
49. Teams ___ excellence from hard work
51. Ticket taker action
54. Abner Doubleday ___ the game of BB, allegedly
55. Rangers Outfielder #3 Leody
59. Standouts on the pitcher's mound
60. College ballers may be on free ___
62. White Sox Pitcher #65 Heuer
63. A broken injury
64. Live dog mascot nose noise
65. How often the Yankees win the WS
66. Electronic ___, one time maker of Triple Play Baseball videogame series
67. Concession offerings
68. Rays Pitcher #29 Fairbanks

Down

1. "G" in GML, which in 2003 was known as the Budweiser League
2. MLB hedging, insur ___
3. Pirates city (short)
4. April for MLB
5. Pitchers good at preventing a score
6. Targeting Pitcher will ___ for the corners
7. "Blue" Jays from owner beer brewer ___ Blue brand
8. White Sox Pitcher #45 Garrett
9. Washington Team
10. Mark made on telestrator
11. Batter crowds plate
12. Rays and Giants water location
14. "Ok" the contract terms
20. Injured Reserve
22. Cleared from a game field, pre-construction
25. MLB players flying first-class
26. Common bone / spinal baseball injury
27. Sit on the bench, AKA ride-the-___
29. Astros Pitcher #48 Paredes
31. "Makes up" a team
34. Tailgate BBQ rack of
35. Inter County Baseball Assoc.
36. CAN has one ___, MLB
38. Phillies Closer #50 Héctor
41. Going to 3rd, turn back to 2nd
43. Yankees "NY"
44. Off center logo area on many jerseys
47. Yankees Pitcher #80 Luis
49. WS parade pageantry, short
50. A ball game is a type of what?
52. HOF Arky Vaughan
53. Announcer summary of the game
54. Dallas Amateur Baseball Assoc.
56. Actor Charlie Sheen as Ricky "Wild Thing" Vaughn in Major League movie
57. A mark made on telestrator
58. Stadium land "spot". Also, MLB.com
61. MLB online ___ com

PUZZLE 24

Baseball Fact: The New York Yankees have won 27 World Series titles, the most in baseball.

Across

1. Heal mark from turf skinning injury
5. MLB HQ meeting, by ___ only: Abbr
9. Announcer summary of the game
14. Central Ontario Baseball Assoc.
15. Bottom of Baseball shoe
16. Waft of concession offerings
17. Hot indoor stadium (slang)
18. Hit, AKA as in "Hit one to the R side"
19. Home plate to 1st base, in chalk
20. Thrown ball at high-speed, like it is from a shooter (slang)
21. High up seats (slang)
23. Bobbled ball, run scores
26. Holds concession food in transit
27. A 18 (ticket, example)
30. Texas Baseball Club
33. MLB in the terms of league status
35. Team logo, crest
36. Pirates AA team locale, Penn
37. Thrown to wrong base, error AKA
39. Pitchers Feller, Lemon & Gibson
40. Runner leaves 3rd to
41. Lebanon Youth Baseball
42. Drunk fan walk
44. Adequate condition of trading card
45. Hit helmets have these
49. Aging player's foe (parental, slang)
55. Arizona Diamondbacks on a scoreboard
56. Cubs most hits: 2995
57. Atlantic Collegiate Baseball League
58. Signs a contract
59. Business interests in a team
60. Uniform shoe tie
61. A base AKA
62. Lots of fouled-off pitches, does to a Pitcher
63. Scully's voice heard on this LA radio station
64. American League Division Series

Down

1. Player Injury examination device
2. Tarp action. Also, Stadium roof purpose
3. Minnesota Twins Mascot
4. Offensive player action from e.g. 1st to 2nd
5. MLB Players ___ : Abbr
6. Early N.Y. Giants field, ___ Grounds
7. Many modern stadium's façade, material
8. Cubs Pitcher #18 Ryan
9. Cardinals famous squirrel meaning
10. CLE Indian's Great Lake
11. 5x WS, 5x All-Star, '94 Cy Young "pylon" P
12. Indians Outfielder #1 Rosario
13. San Diego Padres NN
22. In an offensive box
24. Baltimore Orioles NN
25. A's Pitcher #54 Sergio
28. Detroit's Canadian city neighbor, Ontario
29. Mariners city on a scoreboard
30. CAN has one ___ in the MLB
31. Players and fans, like a cake in hot sun (slang)
32. Cleveland on the scoreboard
33. A team's cunning trade plan
34. Round Tapered Baseball Bat
35. Stadium seller of merch
36. Australian Baseball League
37. Drink container, from concession
38. Grass crews equipment storage place
40. "Extreme" change needed for bad teams
43. Play-by-play's job is
44. Griffey Sr. passed on to Griffey Jr.
46. National Assoc. of Prof, Baseball Leagues
47. Injury cart field mark
48. Anthem leader does it
49. BB's pace of play, not so much
50. MLB has been accused of ___ trust
51. MLB Comish AKA (slang)
52. Player is acting, not injured
53. Massachusetts Baseball Coaches Assoc.
54. Night games need this power (short)
58. Like some batteries & baseball leagues

PUZZLE 25

Baseball Fact: An easy fly ball is called a "can of corn". The term comes from grocers using their aprons to catch cans knocked from high shelves.

Across

1. Old stadiums like OAK's haven't done it well
5. Action to get names on trophy
9. Uniform's are from of it
14. NN "Charlie Hustle", Pete
15. Sonic maker & Fr. maker of top MLB VG
16. Single-A ball, upper division name
17. Response from player that messed up
18. Tacoma Rainiers Baseball Network
19. Phillies St. Pitcher #56 Zach
20. An organization of teams & leagues
22. Distraction plays
24. Practice squad player
25. Indians Pitcher #78 Morgan
26. "Interpret" the signal
27. New York Mets NN
32. Eight ___ dozen balls used in a typical game
34. Pitcher may have ___ 100+ by game's end
35. Effect on ball of a knuckler
36. Slide pen ___ along paper to sign contract
37. 1993 AL Batting Champ, John
41. Mets Owner/CEO – Steve
44. Games that baseball became official in '92
46. Stats
47. Earned run average
48. Players winning WS do it, together
52. Royals Mng 1987, 62W-64L record
56. Looked for pitch, got it
57. May be seen from serious injury
58. Concession action, to make drinks
60. Term for a # besides 0 or 1 on a scoreboard, ___ crooked
61. Player Injury examination device
62. European Baseball Coaches Assoc.
63. Contract upping
64. "Requested" trade
65. Nationals Catcher #38 Barrera
66. Throw

Down

1. Fan's lion-like reaction
2. A coach's is cooked if he loses
3. Sports athletes & writers awards
4. Ice cream from concession
5. Yankees Outfielder #90 Florial
6. Protective cup is ___ a jock strap
7. Cottage Grove Baseball
8. Twins Pitcher #57 Robles
9. Fans do with their top baseball card
10. A win lends this to a dying team
11. Fans "stare" at pro players
12. Margin of error, when similar level teams compete
13. "Honus" Wagner AKA
21. Cleared from a game field, construction
23. Bruising injury, major side effect
28. HOF Mariano Rivera
29. Error made by the pitcher
30. ___ Killing, AKA double play
31. Sunday Night Baseball
32. Bridge type btw Athletics and Giants ($)
33. Team's should, regarding league rules
35. Ghostly noise from a mad fan
38. Rob Manfred, Comish
39. Infielder gets hit by sliding runner
40. Straights of a $$$ struggling league
41. Captures the game
42. Olmsted Travel Baseball Assoc.
43. Player's helmet
45. Another term for turf
46. Too little info from game 1 to ___ anything
49. Braves Pitcher #72 Víctor
50. Hundreds needed to buy game ticket
51. All are checked by BB card grader
52. Grandview Baseball Softball Assoc.
53. American League Champ. Series
54. 1st year player (short). Also, chess piece
55. MLB tests its players for it
59. Official Baseball Rules

PUZZLE 26

1	2	3	4		5	6	7	8		9	10	11	12	13
14					15					16				
17					18					19				
20				21			22	23						
24							25							
		26					27			28	29	30	31	
	32	33						34						
35												36		
37			38	39	40				41	42	43			
44					45		46							
			47				48				49	50	51	
52	53	54	55				56							
57					58	59				60				
61					62					63				
64					65					66				

Baseball Fact: The record # of innings played in an MLB game was 26 on May 1, 1920, when the Brooklyn Dodgers played the Boston Braves.

Across

1. Dishonest Umpire, may be on the ___
5. MIA and TB foliage
9. Ontario Senior Baseball Assoc.
13. If Pitcher does it after motion, it causes a balk
14. How often the Yankees win the WS
15. Stadium brew
16. Error made by the right fielder
17. A team's is, to keep playing in October
18. Concession fries sprinkling
19. Games time estimations: Abbr
20. Term for fielders throwing carefully, often underhanded e.g. 1B to P
21. Red Sox Infielder #36 Hudson
22. "Good Old Ball Game"
24. South Brooklyn Baseball League
26. Your team wins all games, cleanly
29. Red Sox Pitcher #48 Colten
33. Baseball Federation Of Japan
36. ___ the strike zone (weapon)
38. Blue Jays Pitcher #60 Ty
39. 1980 AL MVP
41. Scary noise from an angry fan
42. 2016 Wilson Defensive POY
43. Conseco was 1/2 of this A's brother duo
44. Natural ball grease
46. Torre Baseball Training
47. Pre game player's formal what?
49. MLB to be ___ on ESPN through to 2021
51. Concession offerings
53. A pitch that breaks over the plate
57. Team is hot, scoring run after run
60. Coaches helper (short)
63. Closest of a close play, adverb
64. Messy locker room occupant
65. Players faces on TV HUD (short)
66. Orioles Infielder #41 Tyler
67. Foreign player needs one to play in USA
68. Play-by-play does it a lot
69. Red Sox Pitcher #31 Austin
70. Teammate AKA
71. All Star Baseball Academy
72. Old moldy stadiums

Down

1. Extra inning
2. Clemens was deemed one, regarding PEDs
3. Twins AA team state
4. Shades protect them from the sun (sl.)
5. Has sports writing on it
6. Eases hot summer day sunburn
7. Struggling pitcher does to all bases
8. Montreal Expos, as was seen on scoreboards
9. Old stadiums, no longer useful
10. Fan butt goes here
11. Holds up baseball player's pants
12. Electronic ___, fr. maker of MLB Triple Play baseball video game series
13. Ball hit far into OF
20. Players are above 6, usually
21. Prep Baseball Report
23. Bat the ball like a hit to a fly
25. Basketball Baseball Kickball, league
27. East Toronto Baseball Assoc.
28. Nationals Pitcher #30 Espino
30. Rangers most walks allowed: 1001
31. Elite Championship Tournament Baseball
32. Pitchers between starts
33. Big Bad Baseball Annual
34. Party house of college baller
35. "Joke" between teammates
37. Contract "money" (slang)
40. Twins Pitcher #56 Caleb
42. Abandon the previously agreed on pitch
44. Pitcher does to his position, pre pitch
45. Yankees reach area for fan base
48. Chapman, only player hit by pitch, then die
50. 2003 ALCS MVP
52. Thrown overhead of intended target (slang)
54. Twins Pitcher #31 Smeltzer
55. Nationals St. Pitcher #23 Fedde
56. Nationals Pitcher #33 Harper
57. Season ticket offer stipulation
58. Muscled player denying PED use is this
59. Score less result
61. Turf burn heal mark
62. Springfield Southwest Baseball Assoc.
65. Poland Baseball Assoc.
66. National Baseball Day

PUZZLE 27

Baseball Fact: The longest game was 8 hrs 6 min over 25 innings between the Chicago White Sox & Milwaukee Brewers on May 9, 1984.

Across

1. Stadium place with team merch
5. Austin Metro Baseball League
9. No games day, teams are what?
12. Braves Outfielder #13 Ronald, Jr.
13. Cubs Pitcher #80 Abbott
14. Brookwood Athletic Assoc. for Baseball
16. HR. Also, a Simpson
17. Players needing cardio go for ___
18. Brewers Catcher #9 Manny
19. High hit ball launched into (slang)
20. Red Sox AA team locale, Portland
22. Fan reaction to a bad play. Also, Coach when confronting Umpire
23. 2016 WS MVP Zobrist & Twin CF #11 Revere
24. An OAK baseball follower
27. Has tickets, will part w them
29. Helmet side opening
31. Anaheim Angels on scoreboard
32. Cardinals City
33. Batter does when in the box
36. Every team strives to play for it
37. Infielder may be, when hit low by sliding baserunner
39. Concession baked goods
40. Press is looking for a player to be "honest"
41. A too drunk, belligerent fan risks this
45. Braves Outfielder #11 Inciarte
46. Cheap tickets may ___ fans to the game
48. Player must dress this way, pre game arrival
50. Many players enter camp out of ___
52. Attendance turn counter
53. An Apple brand game streaming device
56. Investors "looked at" the franchise opportunity
57. White Sox Senior Executive VP
58. Texas Elite Baseball Assoc.
59. Indians Catcher #46 Rivera
60. Tigers St. Pitcher #62 José
61. Performance Enhancing Drug
62. Numbers that gamblers want to know
63. Pitchers between starts

Down

1. Check MLB.com for them
2. A classy loser's demeanor
3. 1994 AL Batting Champ
4. 4 innings of a game is only what?
5. Captures the game
6. Pirates Outfielder #19 Colin
7. Minor injuries caused by rough baseball play
8. White Sox St. Pitcher #33 Lance
9. On Base Percentage
10. Foul lines indicate ___ or ___
11. Seat filler
12. Pirate's mascot's greeting
15. Red Sox Closer #19 Matt
21. Arrive "before" (than) 1st pitch is thrown
23. Marlins Pitcher #80 Anthony
25. Hard gunned hit
26. "No MLB players take PEDs" is what?
28. Early 1900s AL pre-Yanks NYC team, the High___
30. What player's have on
33. Pitched ball rotation AKA
34. Although said to be 2 evenly matched teams, many WS games ___ one-sided (3wd)
35. MLB hedging, insur ___
37. Batter does with the bat for hitting
38. Rain caused the game to be
39. Tigers Infielders #19 Isaac
42. 9 innings of a game, usually
43. Team "grabs, captures" and holds the lead
44. The players AKA
47. Sliding runner will, if hits infielder low
49. True Earned Run Average
51. Pitcher that wins them Game 7 of WS
52. Common bone / spinal baseball injury
54. Coach encouragement, talk type
55. Ken Griffey Sr. is to Jr.

PUZZLE 28

Baseball Fact: The modern-day record for the least number of fans was Florida Marlins vs Cincinnati Reds in 2011. Due to Hurricane Irene, only 347 people attended live.

Across

1. Springfield Southwest Baseball Assoc.
5. Team w salary surplus, can for Free Agent
11. Baserunner, advance on his own
12. Runner made it to 1B before the throw
14. Press will, regarding a player scandal
15. Player's bone injury
16. NL Rookie 2019
17. Pitcher off day
18. Player's girlfriend
19. Reaction tasting stadium hot-dog
20. Player garb during late fall game
21. Western Hemisphere Baseball League
22. Traveling teams need to know: Abbr
24. Revenue level of no-win teams
25. Orioles Pitcher #51 Fry
26. The fan mail was ___ through USPS
27. Attempts (short)
28. Credit card for tix, action
29. Amateur Baseball Federation of India
31. Netherlands born, 20 season Fr. Twins Pitcher, Blyleven
32. Trade discussions "brought up" after bad game
34. Players in the dugout
35. Modern and pre-modern pro baseball times
39. 1B "Marvelous" Throneberry, appeared in Miller Lite commercials in the 1970s-80s
40. Tops stadium drinks
41. Pitcher's shoulder muscle injury (short)
42. Cinematic game capture (camera)
43. Players go for them for cardio
44. Thornton Baseball Assoc.
45. MLB…. An "Organization" of 30 teams, short
46. Shop with memorabilia
47. One who scores
50. Even scoring games
52. Documents game details, also news
53. Sliding players regularly get bumps and ___
54. Shoe nub
55. Help with the defensive play
56. Players sunglass appearance

Down

1. Mets St. Pitcher #0 Marcus
2. Mets Pitcher #61 Reid-Foley
3. Marlins Pitcher #52 Anthony
4. Shea stadium, 1974-75 home to Mets & ___ Yanks
5. All-Star game in July, for most players
6. Eat a lot at the game
7. Stat in the record book
8. 21 year Giant, "Master Melvin"
9. "Scuff up" the ball, w dirt or sand paper
10. Cal Ripken as a player, description
11. Four-fingered, means intentional base on balls
13. Announcers do it all game, about the game
14. Wesley Snipes 1989 "Major League" movie character Willie Mays ___
15. Uniform buttons location
20. New York Mets stadium
21. "Lined up" before using restroom
23. Stadium climb obstacles
24. Common Umpire call
25. HOF Pee Wee Reese
28. Completed trading card collections
30. Baseball Softball Verband
31. Investors submit initially, to gain franchises
32. 29 MLB teams play here
33. Arlington Team
34. Catcher fingers, when pointed downward
36. IFs when batter rescinds bunting stance
37. Mets Outfielder #4 Almora
38. Houston Astros NN
40. Single A of affiliated leagues, teams
42. Amount of beers drank at any game
43. Angels Pitcher #49 Hoyt
46. Big ___, David Ortiz NN
47. Strikeout Rate, calculate-able stat
48. 5 MLB team state (short)
49. If stadium entrance is accessible
51. High-velocity fastball

PUZZLE 29

Baseball Fact: The 1st radio broadcast of an MLB game happened on August 5, 1921, by KDKA in Pittsburgh. The 1st place Pirates beat the last place Phillies 8-5 at Forbes Field.

Across

1. Old stadium roof, black covering
4. Numbers that gamblers want to know
8. "Rake" the infield dirt
12. Pitcher's arm post-game
13. Coach goes on about team's lousy performance
14. Nationals Catcher #6 Alex
16. 2B - 3B, short
17. MLB website provides it (short)
18. New England Collegiate Baseball League
19. The blimp over the stadium
21. IFs when batter rescinds bunting stance
23. Hit well, solid AKA
24. Players and their old teams
25. End of bat, billiard hit
26. Error made by the center fielder
31. Post game question askers
33. A's Pitcher #54 Romo
34. Opponents Batting Average, stat
35. Baseball Card World
36. A break during practice, like school
40. "Hit" for extra bases or HR (slang)
43. Portion of 50-50 tix rev. ___ charity
44. Team is on-fire
45. American Baseball Network
47. Condition that ends game prematurely
51. Steroid use and MLB rules
55. Too small for a new stadium
56. No-nonsense Coach during presser
57. Players & fans do it in the summer sun
59. Game on, beer in
60. 50-50 tix, a type of
61. Spot of the stadium
62. Baseball movie's story
63. Manager of the NYY, Aaron ___ e
64. Indians Outfielder #1 Rosario
65. CAN MLB TV show'er

Down

1. Put together scores
2. "A part" in a baseball movie
3. Swap a player for another
4. Baltimore Team
5. White Sox Infielder #20 Mendick
6. Did Not Finish, game status
7. Stadium merch seller
8. Obstructed seat negative
9. Game is at its "end"
10. Critters running around old stadiums
11. Big Lake Baseball Assoc.
12. South Shore Baseball Club
15. Back up position player (short)
20. H___ Wagner, valuable baseball trading card
22. League directors (short)
27. HOF Ivan Rodriguez
28. Greensboro Grasshoppers Baseball Network
29. KC fan to bigger city fan (derogatory)
30. Players are expected to ___ the line
31. Prof. Baseball Employment Opportunities
32. Pennant competition
34. MLB.... An "Organization", short
37. HOF Enos Slaughter
38. Yankees Outfielder #27 Giancarlo
39. Upset fan after team's WS loss
40. Tickets at the entrance
41. Tiger crowd when team takes the lead
42. Cub fan, Bartman - interface "catch"
46. North Thornton Baseball and Softball Assoc.
47. Stadium bins are for what?
48. Team move to a new city, needs a few U-___
49. "Taunt" the Pitcher to scramble his play
50. Pitchers between starts
51. Australian Baseball League
52. Cheese on stadium nachos
53. Pro player operates an expensive one
54. 100 wins can get you ___ the playoffs
58. Offense's ___ is to score

PUZZLE 30

Baseball Fact: Eddie Gaedel was the shortest player to take a bat in MLB. At 3 feet, 7 inches tall, he was part of a publicity stunt for the St. Louis Browns vs Detroit Tigers on August 19, 1951.

Across

1. Seattle is ___ team, most years
5. Needed after long, tiring game
9. Old time word for bat
14. Hank Aaron, born in Mobile ___ (slang)
15. Runner btw the Catcher & Third Baseman is in one
16. Sharp triangular part of player's shoulder
17. Gamblers make one on a game
18. Team owner does for public funding
19. Fat players jerseys
20. MLB team may do for city revenue
22. Stat columns, "organized"
23. MLB tries to with fans
25. A's Catcher #37 Garcia
29. Water sources on the bench
34. Home team is, to the city, residents
35. Hard gunned hit
37. Error made by the pitcher
38. TP, Triple ___
39. Fans do from the stands at poor playing team
40. Nippon League continent
41. Player that hits game winning HR
42. VIP threw ceremonial 1st pitch, 1910
43. Blue Jays Pitcher #57 Thornton
44. MLB streaming service, device type
46. A team of untidy players
47. After game talk with media
50. Old style pants exposed these muscles
54. A Diamond's is an even shaped ___ ogram
59. Concession rings
60. American International Baseball Club
61. Watching the game in the stadium
62. NY to the Yanks
63. Cleared from a game field, construction
64. Pro declining in talent, dread becoming has ___
65. Unlike NFL, MLB games are not on one
66. Foul "territory" (short)
67. Visiting team's accommodations

Down

1. A base AKA
2. Ruth
3. Pre game prayer, ending
4. Schedule number
5. AB
6. Royals career most games: 2,707
7. Known base stealer with long lead off
8. "Twin killings" in baseball: Abbr
9. Cubs Pitcher #80 Cory
10. Speech after pitch to the head
11. The player strike put a sudden ___ to the season
12. Star player may live on it, fall off of it
13. Team owner may also be stadium ___ holder
21. How major leaguers travelled, early 1900s
22. Royals Pitcher #58 Barlow
24. Basket catch, glove at waist "ish"
25. Baseballer and pro athlete, male type
26. 2010 NL Gold Glove 3rd Base
27. Trading refers to a player or ___
28. City celeb option for opening pitch
30. Team lost a big game, reaction
31. A bad team does it often
32. Error made by the right fielder
33. Fans are assigned to them
35. Purpose of the brim on a BB hat
36. Hall Of Fame, Cooperstown NY
39. Press does w player controversies
43. True Earned Run Average
45. First game of season
46. Nationals Infielder #27 Jordy
48. A pyramid structure on a stadium
49. Well-known baseball research - ___metrics
50. Ticket set back
51. MLB has been accused of ___ trust
52. White Sox Closer #31 Hendriks
53. HOF selection process
55. Little League Baseball Incorporated
56. By not making stadium payments
57. 2 and 2 count
58. Players vision correction tool
60. Attempts (short)

PUZZLE 31

1	2	3	4		5	6	7	8		9	10	11	12	13
14					15					16				
17					18					19				
20				21				22					
				23			24						
25	26	27	28				29			30	31	32	33
34					35	36				37			
38				39					40				
41				42				43				
44				45				46				
			47			48	49					
50	51	52	53				54			55	56	57	58
59					60				61			
62					63				64			
65					66				67			

Baseball Fact: A pitcher's curveball can
bend in excess of 17 inches from a straight
line towards home plate.

Across

1. True Earned Run Average
5. Throws their best at a batter, ___ the S-ZONE
11. Pirates Infielders #38 Will
12. Major Leagues AKA
14. Trade rumors need one
15. Directly hit at defender (slang)
16. Irate coach can be, from game by Ump
17. Runner walks with, after a sliding collision
18. Pitcher Maglie "The Barber" of the 1950s Giants
19. Back up position player (short)
20. Pitchers do, late in the game
21. Some players indulge in the organic (slang)
22. Measurement on OF walls e.g. 330
24. Blue Devils school, 3x ACC champs
25. Unsightly injury, usually with blood
26. Low cost agency desired by player
27. Finger # means fastball
28. Stadium security check of fan
29. 16yr Cub great, "Ryno" Sandberg
31. Game day draft topper
32. More than one contest
34. Red Sox city on a scoreboard
35. Calm fan disapproval
39. Periods, eras or ___ in baseball
40. Red Sox vs Yankees games, militarily
41. Twins most strikeouts: 178 (2016)
42. Bad team, descriptor
43. Cubs as common Reds Opening Day opp.
44. Brewers city on a scoreboard
45. Arizona Diamondbacks: Abbr
46. Opening game field, ideally
47. Pirates Pitcher #55 Chasen
50. Easing pitcher does it
52. Team with most wins so far
53. Nationals Infielder #13 Castro
54. Brewers Infielder #2 Luis
55. Personnel exchanges
56. Teams really ___ on their ace pitcher

Down

1. Players agents, for investments
2. Batting helmet holes exposes them
3. Twins most singles: 182 (1925)
4. Old stadiums like OAK's haven't done it well
5. Pre game player's formal dressing
6. Indians most HR, 337
7. A Cubs non baseball concern in early season (short)
8. All Star Baseball
9. Royals AAA team name, Storm ___
10. A's Pitcher #21 Adam
11. Where tailgaters store the beer
13. West Little League Baseball
14. Team support system
15. BB appeals to young and old fans ___
20. "Take me out to the ball-game"
21. Winning team does with trophy
23. Protective cup is ___ a jock strap
24. 23yr Dodger Sutton & 14yr Yank Mattingly
25. Ground Rule Double
28. Made of star player
30. Contract agreement
31. Stat column organization
32. Reds Pitcher #50 Amir
33. Marlins Infielder #24 Jesús
34. 1st and 2nd are what?
36. Double Header games happen when?
37. Slices concession foods
38. Royals Outfielder #12 Jorge
40. Stadium washroom type
42. Popular MLB sponsor type
43. Baseball big screen portrayal
46. Team did with lead all game long
47. Speech after pitch to the head
48. Team meeting confirmation
49. Team travel method in the early 1900s
51. Inherited Runs Allowed, stat

PUZZLE 32

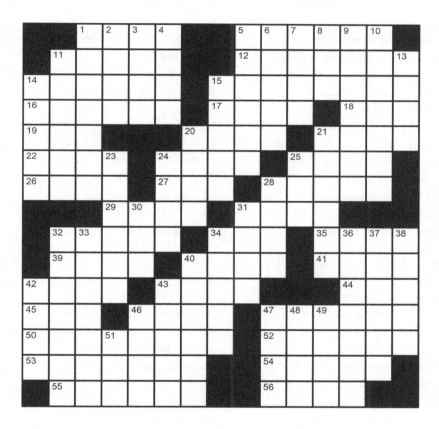

Baseball Fact: The most well-known sale in baseball history was in 1919 when the N.Y. Yankees paid Boston $125,000 for Babe Ruth.

Across

1. MLB Comish AKA (slang)
5. Pacific Palisades Baseball Assoc.
9. Pirates Outfielder #19 Colin
14. Ruth
15. Group of players, like sheep
16. Nationals Catcher #6 Alex
17. Old stadium, no more tenant(s)
19. Announcer summary of the game
20. 3rd jersey AKA
21. Popular pro-player pendant
22. Dodgers SS great Harold Reese NN, Pee ___
23. Fans excitement ___ after a loss
25. Pitcher motions arm back
29. "May I have a beer, ___"
33. Teammates do to Pitcher after a no-hitter
34. Team performance level, high-mountainous
36. Most common nickname for a Pitcher
37. Innings played, stat
38. A's Pitcher #36 Yusmeiro
40. Shoe tighten action
41. New, unheard of sports news
44. Stadium food place
45. 2016 WS MVP Zobrist & Twin CF #11 Revere
46. Time spent coaching a team
48. Orioles Outfielder #24 DJ
50. MLB does for PEDs
52. Device to hit the ball
53. Drink container, from concession
56. Rules not in the book
62. A's Infielder #17 Andrus
63. USA has twenty ___, MLB
64. Players must, by the MLBPA rules
65. East Coast Baseball Academy
66. Round Tapered Baseball Bat
67. Player on the bench
68. Chicago White, Boston Red, named for (sl)
69. Fan reaction to a big play

Down

1. Trojan Baseball Alumni Assoc.
2. South Augusta Baseball League
3. Offense tool
4. A contract do-over
5. Buy tickets through mobile exe
6. Rays highest slugging %: .627, (2007)
7. Fr. 2B, 3x All-star ___ Boone
8. Players from drafts, to roster
9. Braves Outfielder #20 Ozuna
10. A coach does to the team
11. Puerto place, pre season games
12. "We tried but ___, we lost"
13. CLE Indians, known as what in 1903-14?
18. Rays Pitcher #85 Strotman
24. Innings Pitched
25. Good & erratic knuckler (slang)
26. 2 outs, baserunners ___ contact
27. Rays Pitcher #21 Cody
28. They get your other ball-game tickets
30. "Post" game
31. Time in the majors
32. Used to watch a game
33. Stadiums by the bay, sight obstruction
35. Each Savannah Bananas player wore one in 2018 St. Patrick's Day game
39. Same score after 9 needs one
42. Ball is off plate, to the far side of batter
43. After game talk with media
45. Pitcher and the Catcher form it
47. HOF Enos Slaughter
49. 2nd stringers do it for an opportunity
51. Heard during batters intros
53. Steroids (slang)
54. Little League Baseball International
55. Loyal, regular fan
57. Cubs Infielder #2 Hoerner
58. Westminster National Baseball Classic
59. Orioles Pitcher #55 Dillon
60. East Metro Baseball League
61. North Shore Baseball League

PUZZLE 33

Baseball Fact: In 1931, Chattanooga Lookouts of the Southern Assoc. SS Johnny Jones was dealt to the Charlotte Hornets in exchange for a 25-pound turkey.

Across

1. Company messages in stadium (short)
4. High School BaseBall
8. Northeast Adult Baseball League
12. Cleat
13. Team behind in stadium payments risks
14. MLB will be ___ on espn through to 2021
16. NE state cheers for Red Sox as well (short)
17. Orioles St. Pitcher #64 Kremer
18. Red Sox AA team locale, Portland
19. Concession food consequence
21. Hit by pitch, like power tool
23. Yankees "NY"
24. Gets in the Outfielders eyes
25. Baseball (slang)
26. Orioles most RBI, RHB: 150 (2004)
31. Wide "selection" of baseball bats
33. Babe Ruth's middle
34. Korean Baseball Organization
35. Game time estimation: Abbr
36. Loan may keep the team-boat ___
40. Stadium AKA
43. Braves most losses: 230
44. Orioles city on a scoreboard
45. MLB Comish, Manfred
47. Choke ___ = losses done beautifully well
51. Yankees Infielder #29 Gio
55. A single as a stat
56. 1st and 2nd
57. Boring baseball announcer
59. Concession fountain drink
60. Completed plate appearance
61. International Baseball League of Australia
62. 2 and 2 count
63. Concession offerings
64. MIA and TB foliage
65. Season tix, holds that seat (short)

Down

1. Overspending league falls deep into one
2. Free Agents ___ return to club, mostly
3. Local person of note for a Nationals game opening pitch
4. Contest of dingers
5. MLB chew and spit sunflower food
6. Baseball Players Assoc.
7. 2003 NL MVP
8. HOF wanna-be
9. Methodical coach
10. Ball at head, player ducks
11. Mark made on telestrator
12. Santa Clara Baseball League
15. Baseball stitching
20. True Earned Run Average
22. 1915-35 Pitcher-turned-slugger of note
27. HOF Jacob Ruppert
28. Pre game prayer, ending
29. Stats
30. Anaheim Angels: Abbr
31. Amateur Baseball Federation of India
32. Player type, back-up. Also, actors "part"
34. Twins AA team locale, state (short)
37. Pitcher's head nod to sign
38. Cops taking away drunk fans
39. An obnoxious fan. Also, a fixer (slang)
40. Astros Infielder #13 Toro
41. Rodents found in old stadiums
42. Marlins Pitcher #57 Hernández
46. Batting Average on Balls In Play
47. Single-A baseball AKA
48. Action may start a bench brawl
49. Orioles AAA team name
50. Cards batting great___ the Man Musial
51. Ultimate Baseball Academy
52. Player earning measurement
53. Springfield Southwest Baseball Assoc.
54. High velocity fastball
58. Lakeville Baseball Assoc.

PUZZLE 34

Baseball Fact: In 1930, Babe Ruth was being paid $80,000, or $1 million in today's money. When asked how he qualified making more than the President, he responded, "I had a better year."

Across

1. Pacific Palisades Baseball Assoc.
5. Fans must leave seat to puff them (short)
9. Tigers Catcher #40 Wilson
14. Felipe or Moises, first name
15. Pitcher & now Dodger Broadcaster, Hershiser
16. A mark made on telestrator
17. Leagues top dogs, execs
18. Game is "over"
19. Astros St. Pitcher #43 McCullers Jr.
20. Twins AA team locale, state (short)
21. A team is, when looking at a top draft pick
23. Players run out of it late in game
26. Astros Pitcher #63 Tyler
27. On-deck batters outlines
30. Combined Shutout, stat
33. Scannable on tickets
35. McGwire facial hair style (short)
36. Yankees St, Pitcher #50 Taillon
37. AL Rookie 2007
39. Rubs for glove
40. Bill from concession food
41. National League Baseball
42. "Head-on" fielder collision
44. Injured easy when playing on turf
45. NL Manager Of the Year
49. Blue Jays AA team name
55. Anaheim Angels on a scoreboard
56. Minnesota Twins Mascot
57. A team's territory AKA
58. Sports reporter, often accused of creating
59. Orioles most triples: 12 (1967)
60. By not making stadium payments
61. A player claims they do not take PEDs it is
62. Networks and game
63. Avg ball game is 3+ hours ___
64. Nationals Infielder #19 Josh

Down

1. Trading cards come in them
2. Cinch design no longer seen on baseball pants
3. Royals Mng 1995-97, 181W-206L
4. Down Under MLB game host (short)
5. White Sox Pitcher #65 Heuer
6. Cal Ripken Jr. is this Man
7. Orioles Highest slugging %: .646 (1961)
8. Player knee support, brace AKA
9. Astros Pitcher #58 Brooks
10. "We tried but ___, we lost"
11. Face to face Coach-Ump may need (sl)
12. Angels have won World Series
13. Grass crew maintenance supply
22. Producing players earn it from fans
24. Est. three needed for a baseball field
25. Anthem amplifiers (short)
28. Fans "root, root ___ the home team"
29. MLB's Great White North Blue Jays: Abbr
30. AL and NL, ___ as the MLB (short)
31. Baserunner dangles a steal-stance in front of Pitcher
32. Organized Team Activity: Abbr
33. Ball at head, player ducks
34. Australian Major League Baseball
35. Tailgate BBQ necessity
36. Marlins Infielder #5 Berti
37. Signs a contract
38. Baller's alma mater's head honcho
40. Indians Outfielder #9 Eddie
43. Player sent to minors hopes for
44. Indians Manager #77 Francona
46. Brewers Catcher #12 Luke
47. Pirates Infielders #61 Cruz
48. Nationals Infielder #45 Antuna
49. Farmington Amateur Baseball Congress
50. International Baseball League of Australia
51. Tailgating BBQ cooking process
52. Player feature hidden under helmet
53. Too old for Little League
54. Did perform anthem
58. PED testing place

PUZZLE 35

1	2	3	4		5	6	7	8		9	10	11	12	13
14					15					16				
17					18					19				
20					21			22						
23			24	25			26							
			27		28	29						30	31	32
	33	34								35				
36							37		38					
39						40								
41				42	43									
			44						45		46	47	48	
49	50	51	52				53	54			55			
56					57					58				
59					60					61				
62					63					64				

Baseball Fact: Some MLB records include Joe DiMaggio's 56-game hitting streak in 1941, Ted William's .407 batting avg in 1941, Barry Bonds' 73 HRs in 2001, & Cy Young's 511 career wins.

Across

1. Canadian Premier Baseball League
5. Hard gunned hit
9. Twins Pitcher #56 Thielbar
14. Hispanic ballers greeting
15. World Amateur Baseball Assoc.
16. Twins most extra base hits: 84 (1964)
17. Visiting team AKA
18. Major injuries, rush to emerg ___
19. Heard during Star-Spangled-Banner
20. Camera controls. Also, TV watchers clickers
22. Yankees "NY"
24. Rangers Catcher #23 Jose
25. CAN has ___ team in MLB
26. 0-0 score
27. Red Sox Catcher #59 Hernández
32. AL Rookie Of the Year
34. Pitch slang - down main ___, over the plate
35. World Baseball Outreach
36. Austin Select Baseball
37. Blue Jays highest batting avg, .307, Roberto
41. To hit a batter (slang)
44. Long-time announcer Vince Scully did it in 2016
46. Team practice for upcoming game (short)
47. Orioles Infielder #14 Ruiz
48. Currently outscoring opponent
52. The game is on "right-now". Also, gift
56. MLB's top licensed money maker
57. Shoe tighteners
58. Cola sponsor
60. Mexican food concession offering
61. AB
62. Twins Pitcher #82 Bailey
63. East Texas Baseball Academy
64. MLB, for more than 115 of them
65. Banana stalk (bat slang) ___ w bad wood
66. Pitcher's shoulder muscle injury (short)

Down

1. A league record lister
2. A type of hitter, long ball
3. Owner puts it on coach after loss
4. Team travel consideration
5. Royals most RBIs: 144 (2000)
6. Blue Jays most earned runs, 129 (1996)
7. Old Baseball Cards
8. Rangers Pitcher #52 Hearn
9. Games on MLB network
10. How often the Yankees win the WS
11. Stadium beer option
12. Records are for the best ___
13. Marlins Pitcher #52 Anthony
21. Old tech game/TV recorder
23. Baseball HOFer "Slaughter", Bradsher
28. HOF Amos Rusie
29. Fast Fielder body type
30. Sportscaster sits at one
31. Over Thirty Baseball
32. Injured players will play if ___
33. Money from big contract (slang). Also, rioter's action
35. Wins Above Replacement, stat
38. HOF Monte Irvin
39. Cops taking away drunk fans
40. A champion's time, ruling over team-league
41. Practice helps ___ the team for a game
42. Fielders attempt at a high hit ball
43. After refreshing MLB.com web page
45. MLB, online
46. Where a bet goes
49. Player after obvious bad call
50. New England Collegiate Baseball League
51. Players after a win, brag
52. What ballers wanna do every day
53. Experts do for valuing trading card
54. East Coast Baseball Academy
55. Tailgating BBQ cooking process
59. Opponents' Batting Average

PUZZLE 36

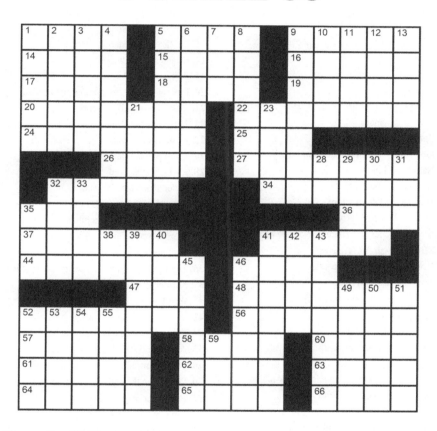

Baseball Fact: George Herman Ruth, Jr. "Babe Ruth" was dubbed "Babe" when another player saw Baltimore Orioles manager Jack Dunn with his fresh new player and said, "There goes Dunnie with his new babe."

Across

1. Longtime Braves great ___ er Jones
5. Colorado American Legion Baseball
9. Old School Baseball League
13. Yankees Manager #17 Aaron
14. Fr. greats Felipe or Moises of MLB
15. Event-less games can be a real ___
16. BB appeals to young and old fans ___
17. "Provoke" a player to get them riled up
18. When MLBPA takes action against MLB
19. Team owner
20. Term for fielders throwing carefully, often underhanded e.g. 1B to P
21. Hits and pushes unexpectant
22. 9 innings of a game
24. South Brooklyn Baseball League
26. TC, ___ Chances
29. Bat diameter, fat at ___
33. First full month of MLB, often (short)
36. Natural ball grease
38. Wraps a bat handle
39. Stadium and dugout tops
41. Isolated Power
42. Royals Pitcher #61 Ángel
43. MLB Comish AKA (slang)
44. How MLB avoids the courts
46. National Baseball League, not assoc w MLB
47. NY Yankee uniform design line
49. Jersey AKA
51. Concession offering
53. MLB award show dress
57. "USA, USA, USA"
60. Team's score with ___ against weak pitcher
63. Inter County Baseball Assoc.
64. Relief pitcher tries to "maintain" his team's lead
65. Greater Victoria Baseball Assoc.
66. Tigers St. Pitcher #29 Skubal
67. Methodical coach
68. Bird mascot has one
69. Anthem heard through a speaker
70. White Sox Catcher #44 Zavala
71. Contract upping
72. Some player's have ___ PEDs, allegedly

Down

1. 2005 AL Cy Young Award
2. WS champs immediately do this with trophy
3. Team, w a pen, does to a deal
4. Dodgers SS great Harold Reese NN, ___ Wee
5. Batting practice area
6. Eases hot summer day sunburn
7. Struggling pitcher does to all bases
8. Sits next to you at the game (short)
9. Old stadiums, no longer useful
10. Players would sell to devil for WS win
11. Fr. 2B, 3x All-star ___ Boone
12. Losers score v winner
13. Ruth
20. Luxury box nacho topping, not cheddar
21. Jackals Baseball Network
23. 2010 NLCS MVP
25. Boston Americans (1901–1907): Abbr
27. "Zero players take PEDs" is what?
28. Roster and injured
30. ___ ed Run Average, stat
31. Newbury Park Pony Baseball
32. Term for delivery of a pitch
33. Degree type of many college players
34. Foul marker
35. Tiger crowds do it after team takes the lead
37. Nationals St. Pitcher #50 Austin
40. Wrigley NN, the ___ Confines
42. Scoreboard display with no runs
44. Fix body inside batter's box
45. A win lends this to a dying team
48. Orioles Infielder #11 Valaika
50. Players go through them at tryouts
52. High School game innings
54. Royals most games: 162 (1977)
55. Jays, Orioles or Cardinals mascot
56. Toronto Blue Jays Ontario water
57. Astros Outfielder #220 McCormick
58. Pitcher does w throwing skills, over time
59. White Sox AA locale, state (short)
61. A batter's tool
62. Nippon League bevy
65. Glasgow Baseball Assoc.
66. Third Base Umpire

PUZZLE 37

Baseball Fact: In 1869 1-time cricket player Harry Wright organized the first pro team, the Cincinnati Red Stockings with 9 players at $950/yr. The Red Stockings' 1st game was Mar 15, 1869, vs Antioch College, winning 41-7.

Across

1. Nicaraguan Professional Baseball League
5. MIA and TB foliage
9. Sports bet AKA
14. Ground Out to Air Out ratio
15. National Bay Baseball Assoc.
16. Dispose of batter quickly
17. "Baltimore's", e.g. team: Abbr. Also, a sandwich
18. College Baseball Coaches Camp
19. A jock protects this on a player
20. Scored less than opponent
21. Oakland on the scoreboard
22. Fans "stare" at pro players
23. Player w allergies oozes it in spring game
26. Pre game prayer, ending
28. Stolen Base Runs
31. Nationals Infielder #45 Yasel
33. Seattle Mariners (since 1977) Pilots (1969): Abbr
36. Yankees Pitcher #63 Lucas
38. Players do it in the dugout
39. Cards batting great, ___ the Man Musial
40. Angels AA team, state (short)
41. No-nonsense Coach is, during presser
43. Passionate emotion for rival team
44. National League Champ. Series
45. Battery type & baseball level
46. 1975 Tiger OTY - 25 HR; 92 RBIs
48. Grand Slam Homeruns, stat
49. Orioles Pitcher #54 Cole
51. Game will, after 9 innings
52. Already watched game
53. California Women's Baseball League
55. Dallas Baseball Academy of Texas
58. Transportation to the game
60. Many a one needed for new stadium
64. Ball grease will do to ball flight
66. Do w team equipment, from city to city
68. Hard gunned hit
69. Fans will after the game ends
70. Eager Beaver Baseball Assoc.
71. 1998 NL MVP
72. All are checked by BB card grader
73. Dallas Amateur Baseball Assoc.
74. New franchise ___ the league a fee

Down

1. National Girls Baseball League
2. Early N.Y. Giants field, ___ Grounds
3. Reds AAA team name
4. A bad team does it often
5. Pittsburgh Pirates stadium
6. Cubs Pitcher #80 Cory
7. Louisiana Baseball Coaches Assoc.
8. Phillies Manager 2015–2017
9. Wild Card Game
10. Mariners Pitcher #41 Fletcher
11. Alcoholic drink from concession (old, slang)
12. Yankees "Empire" NN
13. Indians Catcher #46 Rivera
24. Mild fan harassment
25. Movement/rewarded on a balk
27. Tigers St. Pitcher #48 Boyd
28. Terms such as "dotted", "rifle", "banger"
29. Rays AAA team name
30. When batter tries to hit outside pitch
32. Spit on a ball makes for un___ spin
33. NY to the Yanks
34. White Sox Outfielder #12 Adam
35. Last scheduled game, means the reg. season has come to it
37. MLB Network partner. Hint "T"
39. Solo Home Run
42. Deep hit, like a rocket
47. Baseball (slang)
50. Astros Pitcher #70 Andre
52. Angels Pitcher #40 Cishek
54. Texas team logo design possibility
55. Son of Yogi Berra, 10yr player '77-87
56. Player did from serious injury
57. What a rundown usually ends in
59. Alexandria Area Baseball Assoc.
61. Stadium concession food (slang)
62. NN Charlie Hustle
63. Traveling teams need to know: Abbr
65. Season tix, holds that seat (short)
67. Los Angeles Angels (of Anaheim): Abbr

PUZZLE 38

1	2	3	4		5	6	7	8		9	10	11	12	13
14					15					16			
17					18					19			
20						21				22			
		23	24	25			26	27					
28	29	30		31			32				33	34	35
36			37			38				39			
40					41	42				43			
44					45				46	47			
48					49			50				51		
		52					53			54			
55	56	57				58	59				60	61	62	63
64				65		66			67		68		
69						70					71		
72						73					74		

Baseball Fact: The 1st pro league was the National Association of Professional Baseball Players, 1870 after breaking away from the National Association of Baseball Players, who were still claiming amateurs only.

Across

1. White Sox player, most strikeout to walk, 4.69
5. Free Agents compare them to each other
11. A baseball level below Major
12. "Extend" existing contract
14. Angels best SO to Walk: 2.92
15. Orioles most stolen bases: 57 (1964)
16. Measure the line of balls off bats
17. Team logos, name, print style or typeset
18. Kempsville Pony Baseball
19. Baltimore on the scoreboard
20. Stealing a base is taking a ___
21. Chip partners at WS party
22. Fans "stare" at pro players
24. Injured players will play if ___
25. Cleared from a game field, pre-construction
26. MLB teams can beat semi-pro teams with it
27. If softball is for her, baseball is for
28. WS champs immediately do this with trophy
29. Leagues top dogs, execs
31. West Akron Baseball League
32. Rangers Pitcher #75 A. J.
34. HR balls, distance descriptor
35. Lake Cities Baseball Assoc. (Texas)
39. Slider's jersey appearance
40. Whitey a 16yr Yank, 6x WS champ, 10x All-Star
41. MLB's "suspect" political posturing, 2020
42. Vegas takes, on all leagues
43. Unsightly injury, usually with blood
44. Euro League Baseball
45. Reds Pitcher #77 Warren
46. Ball field location. Also, where children play
47. San Francisco Giants stadium
50. Even scoring affairs
52. White Sox Outfielder #77 Adolfo
53. Sliding players regularly get bumps and ___
54. Old time word for bat
55. Help with the defensive play
56. Rays Pitcher #21 Cody

Down

1. S
2. Methodical coach
3. Fastball sign, finger(s)
4. Pitchers stats
5. Other team to your team
6. Stadium dog
7. Some old stadiums resemble this safe place
8. Rangers Outfielder #41 White
9. Denver Team
10. Bit of sports page article
11. A's Starting Pitcher #55 Sean
13. "Heaps" of concession cheese on nachos
14. Batter is to get on base, AKA ___ setter
15. A baseball "movie"
20. RBI single
21. Practice the basics, over and over
23. A break during practice, like school
24. Pirate's mascot greeting
25. Times On Base, stat
28. Plastic of a helmet
30. Players and their old teams
31. Team is unsure about trade
32. 29 MLB teams play here
33. Yankees "NY"
34. Plastic tool to eat food at stadium
36. Tickets are, at the stadium's entrance
37. Gum wad in a player's cheek
38. Shades color option
40. Material source for bats
42. Reds AAA team name
43. More than one baseball contest
46. Big ___, David Ortiz NN
47. Brewers Catcher #10 Narváez
48. Players always want their pay to do this
49. Post beaned in the head feeling
51. Powers the team bus

PUZZLE 39

Baseball Fact: The most destructive shoulder injury for a pitcher is a labrum tear – tearing of the cartilage. A torn labrum involves surgery, & few pitchers have come back from it the same afterward.

Across

1. Attempts, stat (short)
4. Injured players will play if ___
8. Holds concession food in transit
12. Coach or veteran player, rookie helper
13. A team's support from a bank
14. Yesterday's game, on TV again
16. What a rundown usually ends in
17. Team ID
18. Curveball, AKA ___ Charlie
19. Opening Day game in 2012, 16 innings
21. A team that fails to score in a game does what?
23. A
24. Interference, stat (short)
25. Morganna, Kissing Bandit, other Bball
26. 2013 ALCS MVP
31. Ingredient in many concession drinks, treats
33. Sony's yearly "MLB The Show" video games
34. SS Banner, 3rd word
35. Monday Night Baseball
36. Fly over advertisers
40. April game, fan's skin tone is white as a
43. Pre game player's formal "dress"
44. Action taken between bases
45. Opponents' Batting Average
47. Pro acknowledges crowd
51. Sticky, grip improving substance
55. Shades protects each one
56. Need plenty of this for new stadium
57. New franchise ___ the league a fee
59. Contract upping
60. Red Sox Infielder #36 Hudson
61. League info sent to team this way
62. Mets home, 1960s
63. Many collapsed teams had it
64. MLB Players ___ : Abbr
65. Seen through a helmet hole

Down

1. Pro players operate expensive ones
2. Paying for tickets, exchange (short)
3. Player seen doing this to jock
4. Best of the pros, & a mid-season game
5. Foot errors on grounded balls
6. Game streaming problem
7. Astros Pitcher #48 Paredes
8. Players agents, for investments
9. Indians Catcher #46 Rivera
10. Ball flights, shape
11. Astros Infielder #10 Gurriel
12. League award show
15. CDN MLB TV show'er, Sports ___
20. East Side Baseball Assoc.
22. Expensive trading card, H___ Wagner
27. Home Runs
28. Teams and win "targets"
29. Stadium cost, month to month
30. Austin Select Baseball
31. Stadium fries, sprinkles
32. Team AKA. Also, a team within a team
34. MLBPA's big contract: Abbr
37. HOF Monte Irvin
38. Coaches will, to Ump against a bad call
39. Sioux Empire Baseball Assoc.
40. Tigers Catcher #17 Greiner
41. "Possess" the ball
42. Movement granted on a balk
46. Waft of concession offerings
47. A's Pitcher #70 Jordan
48. A's Outfielder #20 Mark
49. Ball grease to ball flight
50. Bargaining descriptor
51. MLB The Show VG mobile platform, Sony
52. An Apple brand game streaming device
53. Rangers Infielder #30 Lowe
54. Elite Championship Tournament Baseball
58. Rangers Pitcher #63 Benjamin

PUZZLE 40

Baseball Fact: Catchers regularly develop circulatory complications in their hand from catching so many hard thrown pitches. Catchers suffer from many torn menisci.

Across

1. Pirates Outfielder #60 Tom
5. Alamo City Select Baseball
9. A team's roster and injured
14. Baseball book legal ID: Abbr
15. Explosive hit
16. Orioles Pitcher #60 Mattson
17. Off season workout w weights
18. AAA Durham player (Rays affiliate)
19. The "Ray" ref in Devil Rays, pre 2008
20. Backside injury from ground slide
22. Royals St. Pitcher #51 Brady
23. MLB tries to "bring in" fans
25. Press to players, post game
29. Period of less value for BB cards
34. Money for tickets (short)
35. McGwire facial hair style (short)
37. Poor team's request to league
38. Light, mainly done as a sacrifice hit
39. Why players still chew tobacco
40. Cleared from a game field, construction
41. All Star Baseball Academy
42. Brewers Catcher #10 Narváez
43. MLB film holders
44. Sit on the bench, AKA ride-___
46. 2013 NL Manager of the Year
47. Warm up area. Also, animal enclosure
50. White Sox, most sacrifice flies, 109
54. A washed-up player (3wd)
59. White Sox St. Pitcher #55 Carlos
60. Player w allergies oozes it in spring game
61. Oxford Recreational Baseball Assoc.
62. A's are threatening one, again in 2021
63. Dirty helmet sweat may cause
64. Sylmar Independent Baseball League
65. 2019 Wilson Defensive POY
66. Fans "stare" at pro players
67. Turf burn heal mark

Down

1. Each Savannah Bananas player wore one in 2018 St. Patrick's Day game
2. Nippon League continent
3. Amateur Baseball Federation of India
4. MLB player's from outside the US (short)
5. Cubs Pitcher #80 Cory
6. 2 and 2, example
7. Royals most HR: 48 (2019)
8. Baseball Mail League
9. Rosters have them for their player numbers
10. Marlins Infielder #1 Díaz
11. Fans did during National Anthem
12. Orioles Pitcher #55 Dillon
13. Heal mark from turf skin injury
21. Marlins Pitcher #52 Anthony
22. Phillies Infielder #4 Kingery
24. 2 cleats make 1
25. AB, stat
26. Hit ball hard and far
27. It's possible that even though 2 great teams meet in the WS, games ___ lopsided
28. Soda and beer found here
30. Home run (slang)
31. Connected TV cams
32. Angels Outfielder #7 Jo
33. Dodgers SS great Pokey or Pee Wee
35. Pirates Outfielder #18 Ben
36. Opponents' Batting Average
39. Wagner, seen on a very pricey card
43. Scores in baseball
45. Rangers Infielder #77 Andy
46. Fastball AKA
48. White Sox St. Pitcher #33 Lynn
49. Bullpen comms device
50. Runner btw the Catcher & Third Baseman is in one
51. Opening game field, ideally
52. Yankees Infielder #18 Rougned
53. Opening pitch, do with pitch rubber, for celeb
55. Team owner
56. Tigers Catcher #13 Haase
57. Eager Beaver Baseball Assoc.
58. Nebraska American Legion Baseball
60. Pitcher Maglie "The Barber" of the 1950s Giants

PUZZLE 41

1	2	3	4		5	6	7	8		9	10	11	12	13
14					15					16				
17					18					19				
20				21					22					
				23			24							
25	26	27	28					29			30	31	32	33
34					35	36				37				
38					39					40				
41					42				43					
44				45				46						
				47			48	49						
50	51	52	53				54			55	56	57	58	
59					60					61				
62					63					64				
65					66					67				

Baseball Fact: "Soaking" "Patching" & "Plugging",
an early rule that permitted fielders to throw at an off-
the-base player, outing them by hitting them with the
ball. Said to be part of the manliness of the game.

Across

1. Chinese Taipei Baseball Assoc.
5. Gatorade electrolytes may prevent
11. Boston NN
12. A rainy city's stadium roof acts as
14. Oversaw the MLB steroid issue 2005
15. 1/2 way to 1st is the 45 ___
16. Fan feelings toward opposing team's star
17. Convince a player to sign. Also, fishing object
18. MLB Great White North partners: Abbr
19. CAN has ___ MLB team
20. Face to face Coach-Ump may need (sl)
21. HOF Bo Jackson's Nike product
22. Griffey Sr. passed the BB one to Griffey Jr.
24. Paper used to scuff ball
25. Cubs Infielder #9 Javier
26. Numbers that gamblers want to know
27. MLB is an "Organization" (short)
28. Yankees Pitcher #85 Luis
29. Illegal substance in bats for greater distance
31. A great or ___ Fide baseball star
32. Player Injury examination device
34. Backyard Baseball League
35. Kansas Assoc. of Baseball Coaches
39. MLB sponsor type, vroom-vroom
40. Ramsey Baseball and Softball Assoc.
41. International Baseball League of Australia
42. Coach "goes on" about team's lousy performance
43. Sonic maker & Fr. maker of top MLB VG
44. Un-Earned Runs
45. Interference
46. Western Maine Board of Baseball Umpires
47. "Ball through the 5-hole" - references hockey
50. Game info location when watching on TV
52. Measurement of balls off bats
53. Baseball players very first league
54. Camera action, to follow the play
55. Baseball card maker imprints
56. Foul ball identifier

Down

1. Great teams will ___ for the playoffs
2. MLB Comish AKA (slang)
3. Cubs Infielder #13 David
4. Cut from the team
5. A bat-crack, non-visible
6. Stop position
7. Rays Pitcher #29 Fairbanks
8. "Entire" team
9. Jerseys letters, held to cloth with
10. NN of any player hitting .200 or lower
11. Pitcher nailed batter in the head
13. Indians Catcher #46 Rivera
14. Reds Outfielder #4 Akiyama
15. Side-arm throw
20. Equipment logo. Also, ball scuff
21. Mariners most saves: 129
23. Injured player needs one, to get off field
24. Pitcher's arm, shoulder post-game
25. Twins Catcher #70 Rortvedt
28. Concession option
30. On-base Plus Slugging
31. Braidwood Baseball Softball Assoc.
32. Tickets were, electronically, from checker
33. Obstructed seat, problem
34. Very hard line drive AKA
36. A fastball AKA
37. Marlins Pitcher #35 Richard
38. Players emotion about baseball and team
40. 2020 MLB has 10 active - Ol Miss alums
42. Losing team's fan's uncontrolled protest
43. Concession air-born offering
46. Weighted Runs Above Average
47. Baserunner, breath catch noise
48. Alert players jump ___ loose balls
49. Periods, eras or ___ in baseball
51. Challengers Baseball Club

PUZZLE 42

Baseball Fact: In the early version of base ball—at that time 2 words—games were not 9 innings. Clubs played until one side recorded 21-runs, which were termed "aces."

Across

1. MLB does to cheaters
5. Action to imprint names on trophy
9. Indians Closer #48 Emmanuel
14. Injured players will play if ___
15. NorthWest Baseball Institute
16. Mets Infielder #86 Jake
17. Royals Catcher #48 Rivero
19. Stadium AKA
20. Nationals Infielder #13 Castro
21. Base-stealer rockets off with a lot of it
23. Fastball down the middle, a center ___
24. Trading cards, come in
25. Phillies most HR: 548
29. Coach chose not to coach anymore
33. Baseball Think Factory
34. Braves AA team locale, Miss.
36. Broadcasts game happenings
37. Rub for glove
38. Check MLB.com for them
40. Interference
41. Giants Closer, Wilson, famous for it
44. Players from drafts, to roster
46. Over Thirty Baseball
47. Stolen Base Percentage
49. "MLB The Show" Gaming tournaments
51. Celebrating team will dog___ the hero
53. Anaheim Angels: Abbr
54. Umpire decided a play
56. "Head-on" fielder collision
60. TC, ___ Chances
61. Morganna, Kissing Bandit NN
63. Red Sox Pitcher #31 Austin
64. A batter's tool
65. Stadium entrance is accessible
66. How games in the 90s were recorded
67. Player's earning measurement
68. Stadium washroom type

Down

1. Marlins Pitcher #52 Anthony
2. Gamblers make it on a game
3. New Lenox Baseball Assoc.
4. Leagues "hunt" for new talent
5. AL & NL separate, until 2000
6. A Minnesota player
7. MLBPA's big contract: Abbr
8. Trade baits, leaked news, Also, CW clues
9. League membership
10. White Sox Manager #22 Tony
11. Periods, eras or ___ in baseball
12. Player complained, was ___ off
13. Earned Run Average
18. Time of trouble getting hits
22. Not one in the MLB
25. Blue Jays most earned runs, 1091
26. Extra protection on a helmet
27. Collected from gameplay
28. To switch player for payer
30. TV "box" descriptor, for dumb-dumbs (slang)
31. San Francisco Giants NN
32. Night Over Thirty Baseball
33. Pitchers Feller, Lemon & Gibson
35. League corporate structure: Abbr
39. Home and away locker rooms
42. Swap a player for another
43. Hit by pitch, like a power-tool
45. Free Agents ___ return to club, mostly
48. Cleveland Indians: Abbr
50. 50-50 winners chosen by
52. Braves Pitcher #67 Santana
54. Red Sox Manager #13 Alex
55. Mild contact of ball w bat
56. Spectacular play
57. Recording object of baseball's past
58. Pre game prayer, ending
59. Players vision correction tool
60. Torre Baseball Training
62. Rangers Baseball Arlington

PUZZLE 43

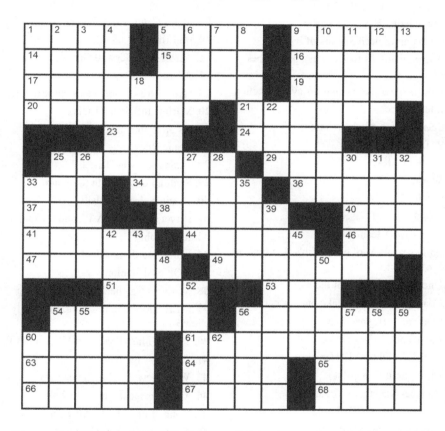

Baseball Fact: Balls have 108 double stiches with the first and last stiches unseen underneath the leather. Some say these double-stitches equates to balls having 216 stitches.

Across

1. Texas Baseball Club
4. Contract upping
8. Holds concession food in transit
12. A team's territory AKA
13. 2014 ALCS MVP
14. TV game from yesterday, shown again today
16. Baseball training facility NN
17. Negotiation benefit (slang)
18. Curve ball AKA ___ Charlie
19. MLB games need 3 hours of it
21. A team that fails to score in a game does what?
23. Players have sun version for eye protection
24. Interference
25. Seen through a helmet hole
26. 2013 ALCS MVP
31. Stadium AKA
33. World ___
34. Catch AKA
35. Monday Night Baseball
36. Twins AAA team name
40. Early season April game, fan's skin tone may be as white as a
43. Unexpected bounce of the ball
44. Coaches tell team to take one for cardio
45. Stadium beer glass edge
47. Pro acknowledges crowd
51. Royals Infielder #49 Hanser
55. Draft qualifier e.g. 1st ___
56. Yankees Manager #17 Aaron
57. Marlins Closer #93 García
59. Nippon League continent
60. 2 outs, baserunners ___ contact
61. 0-0 score
62. Reds AA team locale, state (short)
63. Annie Oakley = Free ___
64. 16yr Cub great "Ryno" Sandberg
65. Shades protect them from the sun (sl.)

Down

1. Behind in score
2. Famous outside the S-Zone hitter, Yogi
3. Obstructed seat problem
4. Captures the game
5. ID on the back of many jerseys
6. White Sox Infielder #7 Anderson
7. Astros Pitcher #48 Paredes
8. Players agents, for investments
9. Indians Catcher #46 Rivera
10. Ball flights
11. Astros Infielder #10 Gurriel
12. A base AKA
15. Games are streamed from here (short)
20. Marlins Infielder #1 Díaz
22. It's up to the player
27. Home Runs
28. Teams and win "targets"
29. Stadium cost, month to month
30. Austin Select Baseball
31. Player's skill btw AAA and the majors
32. RBI double
34. North Seattle Baseball
37. HOF Ned Hanlon
38. Mariners Catcher #22 Luis
39. MLB players do this a lot, especially chewers
40. 1995 Willie Mays World Series MVP
41. "Possess" the ball
42. What crew can do with camera
46. Mariners most wins: 21 (2003)
47. None of them in the MLB, so far
48. Tigers St. Pitcher #12 Mize
49. A mark made on telestrator
50. Coaches devise the strategy & game___
51. Amateur Baseball Report
52. Mets Pitcher #32 Aaron
53. Fide baseball star
54. Baseball HOFer "Slaughter", Bradsher
58. Clinging Boston wood vine in Wrigley

PUZZLE 44

Baseball Fact: A MLB ball must have 2 cowhide pieces laced together with exactly 108 red-waxed cotton stitches, a circumference between 9.00 and 9.25 inches and a weight between 5.00 - 5.25 ounces.

Across

1. Foster City Tournament Baseball
5. Greater Toronto Baseball League
9. A player on a new team with new plays must
14. Player's skill btw AAA and the majors
15. Player type, back-up. Also, actors "part"
16. A bad team does it often
17. Calgary North Baseball League
18. Cal Ripken Jr. is this Man
19. Online baseball photo place (short)
20. Elite Baseball League
21. Reads the news, may include sports
23. Lost after ball hits mouth
26. Tailgating BBQ cooking process
27. Ticket in town, for on-fire team
30. Visiting team transportation
33. Contract detail regarding pay-time
35. Weighted On Base Average
36. Sticky, grip improving substance
37. Tickets for semi-pro, vs MLB
39. MLB hedging, insur ___
40. A fastball AKA, gun ref.
41. Star Spangled Banner, 2nd word
42. Sliding players regularly get bumps and ___
44. Celebrating team will dog___ the hero
45. Coach vs coach "match" (slang)
49. MLB would feel this from a new pro league
55. Games are streamed from here (short)
56. Rangers Pitcher #52 Taylor
57. A "Nick", is often a sign of endearment from fans, teammates
58. Cleats attach to it
59. Indians Infielders #84 Clement
60. Central District Baseball League
61. A rainy game day mishap
62. KC fan, to some (derogatory)
63. 2x WS winner w the Red Sox & only player to hit for the cycle 2x in post season play
64. Pro ball (slang)

Down

1. Strategy is a part / ___ of the game
2. Though the 2 best teams meet in the WS, the game's ___ lopsided
3. Player's job is to get on base AKA ___ setter
4. Baltimore on the scoreboard
5. Players HR facial reaction, minor
6. Player's slide caused uniform damage
7. Loses more games than saves games (slang)
8. Players vision correction tool (pl)
9. Clemens was deemed one, regarding PEDs
10. 23yr Dodger Sutton & 14yr Yank Mattingly
11. Coaches helper (short)
12. Rays Pitcher #29 Fairbanks
13. MLB Comish AKA (slang)
22. Batter's reaction, speed & swing
24. Shout for play at 3rd base
25. Angels Pitcher #49 James
28. Ticket taker, does to ticket
29. Grip improving substance, Pine ___
30. Stars have to with fan attention
31. Gamblers make on a game
32. Set high for teams with stars
33. Brewers Catcher #9 Manny
34. Major injuries, rush to emerg ___
35. Angels Infielder #20 Jared
36. Public Address System
37. MLBPA's big contract: Abbr
38. Night games need this power (short)
40. 2019 NL Platinum Glove
43. Hold onto bat tightly
44. MLB execs deciding rules sit on one
46. Astros Pitcher #48 Paredes
47. Bud, 9th commissioner of baseball
48. Climbed to get to seat
49. Visitors
50. Pitcher that wins them Game 7 of WS
51. Compare players, teams
52. CLE's Great Lake
53. East Metro Baseball League
54. Pitcher's shoulder muscle injury (short)
58. Star Spangled Banner

PUZZLE 45

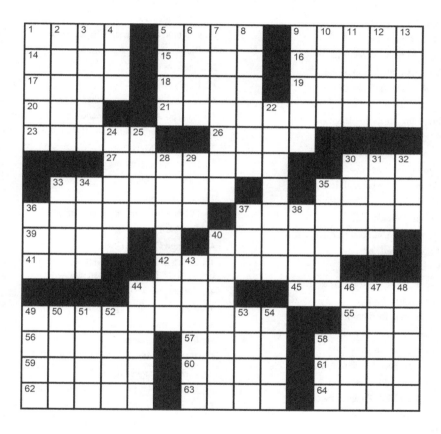

Baseball Fact: The Boston Americans won
pro ball's 1st World Series in 1903.

Across

1. Baltimore "bounce"
5. Holds concession food in transit
9. Soda and beer found here
14. 1/2 way to 1st = 45 ft ___
15. Sparkling, to celebrate after WS win
16. Orioles AA team locale, Maryland
17. Pitcher who kept them off the scoreboard
18. Baseball is round, a football is ___
19. Avoid the tag action
20. Shutout (slang)
22. Stadium type, everyone has a seat
24. Blue Jays Infielders #5 Santiago
26. HOF Old Hoss Radbourn
27. Keeps balls from entering stands. e.g Backstop
28. Pro action to acknowledge crowd
33. Candy from concession AKA
35. Yanks, "Evil Empire" NN is due to
36. Batting Average Against
37. Battery type & baseball league
38. 7x All-Star Lee, & back-flipping Ozzie
42. Indians Infielders #2 Yu
45. Well-known baseball research, Saber___
47. Hard "gunned" hit
48. Observed the play
49. White Sox most stolen bases, 368
53. Concession drink
58. Concession food has a lot of it
59. Listen to the game on it
60. A team's territory AKA
62. National Beep Baseball Assoc.
63. A fan's lion-like reaction
64. MLB's "class" of game is second to none
65. Done for P.E.D.s
66. Premier baseball image depot
67. Pitcher struggled so he was ___ off
68. "We tried but ___ , we lost"

Down

1. Indians Closer #48 Emmanuel
2. Yankees Outfielder #31 Aaron
3. ___ one down
4. H/9, a stat for Hits ___ innings
5. Jays WS wins
6. Red Sox and Yankees, bitter
7. Methodical coach
8. A Pirates color
9. Bench players to gameplay
10. Phillies St. Pitcher #27 Aaron
11. Online baseball announcements (short). Also, dumb player
12. Poor team's request to league
13. Teammate AKA
21. Common twisting, stability leg injury
23. Brewers Infielder #21 Travis
25. Attempts (short)
29. HOF Earl Averill
30. A team acts as one, together. Also, Scottish group
31. What a rundown usually ends in
32. Philadelphia Athletics (1901-54): Abbr
33. Yanks and Mets city
34. Bathroom que, means you
36. Baseman: Abbr
39. HOF Tim Raines
40. Old baseball happenings, documented
41. Turf burn heal mark
42. Chicago Orphans (1901–1902): Abbr
43. 2x WS winner w the Red Sox & only player to hit for the cycle 2x in post season play
44. Braves City
46. Player does on hot game days
47. TV window
50. Royals Outfielder #28 Kyle
51. North Thornton Baseball and Softball Assoc.
52. Fans are assigned to them
53. Infielders ___ toes near base, forced out
54. Tied records after 163g reg season
55. A mark made on telestrator
56. Currency type players are paid in
57. Indian's Great Lake
61. Reds Pitcher #77 Warren

PUZZLE 46

Baseball Fact: The 1st singing of "The Star-Spangled Banner" at a sporting event was in the 7th inning of Game 1 of the 1918 WS between the Cubs & the Red Sox at (rented out) Comiskey Park in Chicago. Sox won 1-0, & the series 4-2.

Across

1. Avg ticket price for MLB games in recent years
5. Baseball broadcaster until 1990s, + s
9. Jeter & A-Rod, diamonds on the diamond
13. Pirates Outfielder #19 Colin
14. Skin tone of Twins fan, early season
15. Mild contact of ball w bat
16. Baseball stadium seating (sl.)
17. Fan's popular alcoholic drink (slang)
18. Louisiana Baseball Coaches Assoc.
19. Vegas takes, on all leagues
20. Lake Cities Baseball Assoc.
21. Indians Pitcher #54 Logan
22. "May I have a beer, ___ "
24. National Bay Baseball Assoc.
26. Players glasses (short)
29. "Spectacular" or magical play
33. A N.Y. player
36. Does the wave during the game
38. Son of Yogi Berra, 10y player '77-87
39. Royals highest batting avg: .390 (1980)
41. From good seats you can ___ all the action
42. Team uniform basic design
43. TB Devil-Ray, a large-bodied one
44. Cubs Pitcher #35 Justin
46. Complete collection of trading cards
47. List of playables
49. Cleared from a game field, construction
51. European Baseball Coaches Assoc.
53. Baseball seam closer
57. Single-A baseball AKA
60. Slider's jersey appearance
63. Great Lake south of Tiger's hometown
64. Mendon Upton Senior Baseball
65. West Akron Baseball League
66. Stadium AKA
67. Peters Township Baseball Assoc.
68. Big League Baseball Academy
69. ___ of land for a stadium
70. Best of the team or league
71. Toronto's mascot movement
72. Skill for statistic calculation

Down

1. On the road player housing
2. Mood of player after a very bad call
3. Twins AA team state
4. Last scheduled game, means the reg. season has come to the
5. Asia Professional Baseball Championship
6. Wire protecting stadium in rough area
7. Solid, unblemished hit
8. Uniform construction
9. Brewers Pitcher w most SO: 1226
10. East Toronto Baseball League
11. Critters running around old stadiums
12. "Length" of game, time
13. MIT Science of Baseball Program
20. Fans "stare" at pro players
21. American Baseball Network
23. Strikeout Rate, stat
25. Minor League travel method
27. Ticket $et back
28. Bat spot providing the best contact
30. Concession offerings
31. "Zero players take PEDs" is a
32. Southpaw Pitcher
33. Make Baseball Fun Again, campaign
34. Brewers Pitcher #52 Lauer
35. Done for P.E.D.s
37. Antler-type spray used as steroid alternative
40. Twins Pitcher #56 Caleb
42. Two teams do it, to play game
44. Ticket seat info (short)
45. Losers score v winner
48. Virtual Baseball League
50. Marlins Outfielder #34 Magneuris
52. On the site of the old Metrodome, for Twins
54. Concession sweet
55. "Tighten" up uniform pants
56. Pitcher's are said to throw it, hot
57. Broadcaster audio equipment need (short)
58. Avoiding inside pitch, batter falls onto
59. All Star Baseball Academy's
61. Eager Beaver Baseball Assoc.
62. Hit, AKA as in "Hit one to the R side"
65. World Baseball Foundation
66. Stadium money giver: Abbr

PUZZLE 47

	1	2	3	4		5	6	7	8		9	10	11	12
13						14					15			
16						17					18			
19					20					21				
22				23				24	25					
			26			27	28		29			30	31	32
33	34	35		36			37			38				
39			40			41			42					
43				44			45			46				
47			48			49			50					
		51			52		53			54	55	56		
57	58	59			60	61	62		63					
64				65				66						
67				68				69						
70				71				72						

Baseball Fact: "Murderer's Row" describes the 1927 Yankee Hall of Famers Lou Gehrig, Babe Ruth, Bob Meusel, Tony Lazzeri, & Earle Combs.

Across

1. Coaching signals
5. Elite Championship Tournament Baseball
9. Team IDs
14. Coaches helper (short)
15. Tiger crowd after team takes the lead
16. Waft of concession offerings
17. Society for American Baseball Research
18. Common sponsor type of MLB, vroom vroom
19. Brewers Pitcher #38 Williams
20. Trojan Baseball Alumni Assoc.
21. Season tix, holds that seat (short)
22. Blue Jays Infielders #72 López
23. Red Sox vs Yankees games, militarily
26. Fr team Montreal Expos, NN
28. Needed for team travel
31. Dodgers SS great Harold Reese NN
33. Riverside Baseball Federation
36. Rangers Pitcher #39 Kolby
38. Angels Pitcher #72 Héctor
39. 5 MLB team state (short)
40. City to city connection
41. Twins Pitcher #41 Anderson
43. "We tried but ___ , we lost"
44. Detroit Tigers NN
45. Condition of many starting training camp
46. Yankees Pitcher #84 Abreu
48. Seasons played by the 1969 MLB SEA Pilots
49. Nationals Infielder #45 Yasel
51. Contract agreement
52. Grounds crew top-dressing
53. Team trying something, maybe sharp
55. PBP - Color guys do it all game long
58. Cools your soda
60. Dirty helmet sweat may cause
64. How shoes are tightened
66. College Baseball Scouting Bureau
68. Stat column organization
69. A corked bat will ___ a ball's flight distance
70. Nippon League continent
71. Inter County Baseball Assoc.
72. Multiple seasons AKA
73. Pirates city (short)
74. Travel team - hotel to stadium movers

Down

1. A baseball movie actors group
2. USA Baseball
3. East Side Baseball Assoc.
4. Early baseball hats
5. Pitcher stat that's better when it's lower
6. Duration of game. Also, where golf is played
7. Orioles Pitcher #55 Dillon
8. Rays Infielder #43 Mike
9. Los Angeles Dodgers on the scoreboard
10. Baltimore Orioles NN
11. Poked the MLB steroid issue in 2005 (short)
12. "Leave/take out" of stats calculation
13. Twins most strikeouts: 178 (2016)
24. First full month of MLB, often (short)
25. A Cincinnati baseball follower
27. ALCS win
28. Mariners Pitcher # 7 Gonzales
29. Poor team's request to league
30. Home ___
32. Mariners Pitcher #40 Mills
33. Astros Pitcher #58 Brooks
34. Anthem heard through a speaker, loud
35. Fisted - Inside ball hits bat near ___
37. Company messages in stadium (short)
39. Visiting team's stadium-hotel transportation
42. Gambling term. Also, a golf specific term
47. Angels on a scoreboard
50. Batter does with the bat for hitting
52. Team's bus driver, action
54. Not fancy, old stadium bench seating
55. Field soil, often 50% sand & 50% ___ mix
56. Phillies Pitcher #41 David
57. Nationals Manager 2007-09, Manny
59. Chatham Baseball and Softball Inc
61. Cola sponsor
62. North Royalton Baseball Boosters
63. Games time estimations: Abbr
65. Defensive Runs Saved, stat
67. What A.L. pitchers normally don't do

PUZZLE 48

1	2	3	4		5	6	7	8		9	10	11	12	13
14					15					16				
17					18					19				
20						21				22				
			23	24	25			26	27					
28	29	30		31			32					33	34	35
36			37			38				39				
40					41	42				43				
44					45			46	47					
48				49			50				51			
			52					53			54			
55	56	57				58	59				60	61	62	63
64				65		66			67		68			
69						70					71			
72						73					74			

Baseball Fact: HOFers Bob Gibson, Lou Brock, & Fergie Jenkins each played for basketball's Harlem Globetrotters.

Across

1. MLB stat
5. Cincinnati Reds Mascot
11. Hear the game on it
12. Marlins Pitcher #57 Hernández
14. Loyal players & time to "give" to team
15. Hot female fan, foot tall attire
16. Phillies Pitcher #77 Medina
17. Pitcher does w throwing skills, over time
18. Earned Run Average
19. Unearned Runs
20. MLB strikeout leader 2019, Gerrit
21. Ball and the wall, for HR
22. Investors "looked at" the franchise opportunity
24. TV cameras have them, power line
25. Weighted Runs Above Average
26. 4 or less innings before rained out?
27. Baseball Performance Training
28. Seen on artistic fan's face
29. Most valuable trading card, a H___ Wagner
31. Fr Catcher, Coach and WW2 spy, Moe
32. Shelburne County Minor Baseball Assoc.
34. Field: Abbr
35. Marlins Infielder #1 Díaz
39. Player is used then dumped (slang)
40. Sports reporter, often accused of creating
41. Mets Catcher #3 Tomás
42. Team, descriptor (slang)
43. Franchise (was in BAL), to N.Y. in 1903
44. A's AAA team locale, state (short)
45. Retired players vs current players
46. Four-run home run, AKA grand ___
47. Players use steroids to gain it
50. Vitamin S, AKA
52. Verbal ask of Umpire, regarding call
53. Beer guy offers a great one
54. Team's tale or back ___
55. Ground ball did this before it stopped
56. Grounds crew watering equipment

Down

1. Gambling term, team likely to win
2. Nationals Pitcher #60 Joan
3. New York Mets stadium
4. Injured easy when playing on turf
5. Most players retire for this reason
6. A mark made on telestrator
7. Dog ___, team celebration
8. Dodgers SS great Harold Reese NN, ___ Wee
9. Yankees Outfielder #90 Florial
10. Players on vacation, from baseball
11. Flight for a busy team
13. Tiger crowd when team takes the lead
14. Orioles fewest strikeouts: 19 (1980)
15. 2B - 3B, stop
20. Needed for WS security, extra
21. N.Y. for the Giants franchise
23. When Leagues run out of $$
24. California Baseball Umpires Assoc.
25. Exaggeration of a very competitive game
28. Performance Enhancing Drugs
30. National Baseball Day
31. Player did from serious injury
32. Dugout roof is a form of
33. Red Sox Outfielder #16 Franchy
34. Baseball "movies"
36. Press is looking for a player to be, when answering questions
37. Rain can cause it
38. "The Natural", baseball story, before movie
40. Baserunners on all three bases
42. Big guy on team, NN
43. Concession pizza serving
46. What is under the grass field
47. To hit a baseball well (slang)
48. WS tickets can be ___ $5k
49. Montreal Expos NN
51. Rancocas Valley semi-pro baseball League

PUZZLE 49

Baseball Fact: Like the U.S., countries Venezuela, Taiwan, Cuba, & the Dominican Republic recognize baseball as their non-official sport.

Across

1. Lewisville Baseball Assoc.
4. Scores
8. Many a one needed for new stadium
12. 50-50 ticket rolled into one
13. A team's territory AKA
14. Reaction to an underdog win
16. MLB teams can beat semi-pro teams with it
17. National Girls Baseball League
18. Concession food, comes w marinara sauce
19. Earned Run ratio
21. Players must ___ the MLBPA rules
23. The game was ___ in the last at bat
24. Defensive Efficiency Rating, stat
25. Transport to the game
26. Location of the pitch, ___ ball
31. Pirates Pitcher w most shutouts: 44
33. "Spectacular" or magical play
34. Los Angeles Angels on the scoreboard
35. League for Youth Baseball
36. "Blue" Jays from owner brewer ___ Blue brand
40. Attempts a steal
43. Blue Jays Pitcher #63 Anthony
44. American Baseball Network
45. Down under MLB game host nation (short)
47. Brewers Outfielder #24 García
51. Field lines, indicators are drawn in it
55. "My bad" self point
56. Indians St. Pitcher #43 Civale
57. Records are for the best ___
59. Games time estimations: Abbr
60. A player's best years. Also, best meat, cuts
61. Brewers Catcher #9 Manny
62. Creative degree type of many college players
63. Team owner may also be stadium ___ holder
64. Trading cards, complete "collections"
65. 2005 Willie Mays World Series MVP

Down

1. Fans will after the game ends
2. Baseball And Softball Enhancement Center
3. Star Spangled Banner, honors what?
4. Arlington Team
5. Fans are, to make noise to inspire team
6. Royals AAA team state (short)
7. Rabbit food at concession
8. Hard to hit fastball (slang)
9. Pirates Pitcher #39 Kuhl
10. Reds most ever hits: 3,358
11. Elite Championship Tournament Baseball
12. Take-in the sports page
15. Blue Jays St. Pitcher #47 Anthony
20. Marlins Outfielder #14 Duvall
22. Reds Catcher #46 Taylor
27. HOF Mariano Rivera
28. Vision to watch game
29. Orioles Outfielder #21 Austin
30. Expos Le Baseball
31. Player's skill btw AAA and the majors
32. Players modern, trendy poses after a HR
34. Many leagues file this way
37. HOF Alan Trammell
38. Anthem, best when a ___ singer performs
39. "Travel" team is on one
40. Rangers Outfielder #3 Leody
41. RBI single
42. #3 will play "in place" of #33
46. Climbed to get to seat
47. Represents a player
48. Gene, singing cowboy actor & original Angels owner
49. Player mood when deemed out from bad call
50. Losers score v winner
51. Stadium Beer and soda comes from it
52. Plastic of a helmet
53. Great Lake south of Tiger's city
54. Covers a stadium
58. "Compete" for title

PUZZLE 50

	1	2	3		4	5	6	7		8	9	10	11	
12				13				14				15
16				17				18				
19			20				21	22					
23						24						
		25				26		27	28	29	30
	31	32				33					
34							35			
36			37	38	39		40	41	42		
43					44				
		45		46		47			48	49	50
51	52	53	54			55				
56				57	58		59		
60				61			62		
	63			64			65		

Baseball Fact: Toronto Blue Jays & Atlanta Braves manager Bobby Cox was ejected a leading 161 times.

PUZZLE 1

SHAM	LAST	HAASE
PINA	OBER	ANSON
OVAL	FREY	ROSSO
SELECTED		MANTAS
	HOUSTON	
TRUMAN		ENGAGED
RERUN	PAST	FOXY
ABET	WORTH	TOPS
DENT	ARTS	PEDRO
ELASTIC		PERSON
	ASHTREE	
TALENT		HARRISON
ALOAN	SODA	COMB
GOOSE	ARIZ	BALB
SUPER	YNOA	APBA

PUZZLE 2

FLAB		AFFORD
DEUCE		BEATOUT
BARREL	FRACTURE
ARREST	REST	GAL
IRA	GOAT	WHBL
TERA	SANK	PAUL
SNOB	ALT	SWIPE
	SOFA	CERT
SCORE	SLC	ERAS
CARB	CHAS	DELT
NRBB	LEON	TBA
BAR	BANG	SCORER
STEPINTO	PAPERS
ACREAGE	CLEAT
HANSER	TINT

PUZZLE 3

KNOT	IPOD	CSPCT
LIVE	CANO	ACTOR
ADALBERTO	TABLE
COLLECTOR	BLADE
EAR	SKIP
GARRETT	CREATE
NATS	AREA	DRAYS
DMB	MIXUP	RIP
BEARD	MATE	SONY
ALTERS	SORTING
DISH	SIX
PRPBL	ONCONTACT
ABALL	SWINGINAS
ISSUE	EBBA	ETBA
RATED	DIAL	SEAR

PUZZLE 4

DEAF	BBBA	TRES
APBA	ARIAS	HIVE
TICE	LANDS	EVEN
ACADEMY	DISBAND
ODOM	OSWALT
INN	REMOTES
TOES	ARI	SPICES
CLOUD	A	TCCBL
HANSER	MLB	SBBA
PREMIER	LAP
SLEEVE	TEAR
BLANKED	TAVERAS
LIND	RIDES	CONE
EDGE	SNORT	ALOE
DEED	EATS	PENN

PUZZLE 5

C	H	A	D		S	E	C	S		S	W	A	B	L
H	A	R	P		C	B	U	A		L	I	M	I	T
A	G	E	S		A	B	E	D		A	B	I	R	D
N	E	N		R	A	L	L	Y	C	A	R	D	S	
G	R	A	S	P		L	E	A	K					
		T	H	E	B	A	R	N			A	B	R	
	A	G	U	I	L	A	R		K		E	R	I	E
S	A	N	D	L	I	N		P	E	A	N	U	T	S
B	A	B	Y		E		B	E	E	L	I	N	E	
A	A	A		S	W	A	N	S	O	N				
		B	E	A	D		T	E	S	T	S			
F	A	T	H	E	R	T	I	M	E			H	A	T
L	A	U	E	R		E	D	U	C		B	A	B	E
A	B	E	A	R		R	E	S	T		O	K	L	A
P	A	S	T	A		Y	A	B	B		R	E	E	L

PUZZLE 6

S	W	A	G		S	H	A	W		B	A	S	E	S
P	A	G	E		T	A	B	A		A	M	O	V	E
A	K	I	N		I	N	N	S		D	I	R	E	C
R	E	N	E	W	E	D		N	E	I	D	E	R	T
E	N	G	R	A	V	E		O	L	D				
		A	G	E	D		T	E	E	B	A	L	L	
	T	Y	L	E	R			C	A	R	D	I	O	
B	E	N								O	C	T		
A	L	O	M	A	R		P	L	U	N	K			
D	E	A	D	R	E	D		P	R	E	P			
		R	I	O		L	E	A	D	I	N	G		
C	L	E	M	E	N	T		A	P	P	A	R	E	L
L	A	C	E	S		C	O	C	A		T	A	C	O
A	T	B	A	T		O	B	E	R		E	T	B	A
D	E	A	L	S		M	A	D	E		D	E	L	T

PUZZLE 7

	B	L	O	W		N	F	B	C		T	E	R	M
P	L	A	N	E		A	R	E	A		H	S	B	A
C	A	S	E	S		M	E	A	L		R	B	I	T
L	I	S	T		J	E	E	R		C	O	A	S	T
B	R	O	W	S	E		D	R	A	W				
	O	N	T	A	P		I	N	S	I	D	E		
O	F	A		A	S	P	A	S	M		T	R	E	A
S	E	L	I	G		P	R	O		R	O	O	F	S
B	E	A	N		S	T	R	I	K	E		N	Y	Y
A	T	B	A	T	S		A	L	I	N	E			
		S	U	B	S			L	O	N	G	E	R	
C	A	B	L	E		A	C	C	T		T	A	X	I
A	L	O	U		K	I	L	O		W	I	V	E	S
R	O	O	M		A	L	U	M		B	R	I	C	E
T	E	M	P		N	S	B	A		L	E	N	S	

PUZZLE 8

	D	A	S	H		C	A	S	H		J	A	W	
C	A	N	H	A		A	B	C	A		L	M	B	A
O	R	T	I	Z		L	E	A	N		W	O	O	D
A	R	U	L	E		L	A	N	D	S		N		B
T	E	N	D		B	I	R	D		P	R	I	D	E
	N	A	T	H	A	N		A	H	E	A	T	E	R
		O	R	G		L	O	C	K	O	U	T		
R	O	L	E	N			T	I	E	R	S			
R	E	T	I	R	E	D		P	E	A				
I	N	T	E	N	S	E		A	L	L	A	R	D	
C	E	A	S	E		C	O	G	S		L	O	O	T
K		V		R	E	E	S	E		O	F	T	H	E
E	P	I	C		R	I	C	A		M	A	T	E	R
Y	A	N	G		I	V	A	N		A	R	E	N	A
T	O	B		C	E	R	T		R	O	N	Y		

PUZZLE 9

```
TERA      TCBEAR
 CRAIG    ROUGNED
SOURCE   BALLGAME
TOSSED   EVIL  HOU
ALT     PAIN  GETS
FEES  NATS  ERIE
FREE  ADS   ADAMS
 REPS   BUDD
 CRIBS  NAB  ETAS
 REEL   ROBB DOLL
LOSS  DIRE    RBI
OCT  SENT  SCORED
THOROUGH  SEVERE
SERVICE   BRENT
 TELLER   CANS
```

PUZZLE 10

```
ROBERTS    PINA
BAL  LOOT  USAB
INITIATOR  MATA
NOVA DEMO  PAINT
DUEL  NAB  CODY
STREAM CLAP NAP
  NBA  HELL AGE
HATEIT   STABLE
COP  ALAB  ETA
UMP  RENO RENDER
TELE  ANA  NADA
STEVE NICK OMIT
OPEN  ALTERNATE
WIND LONE   GOD
NETS  AROSTER
```

PUZZLE 11

```
CABA  AABA TAPAS
BAIL  TREA ABALL
SANO  TERA CESSA
BASEMENT  BOTTOM
   ANAHEIM
HAROLD  FLASHES
AROLE CALL  TAFT
YULI SOLIS ALIE
ELEV HOTN GROVE
SENATOR   LESSER
   ROSARIO
ACHEAT  NONGAMER
BOARD CODI  CAPE
ERNIE ANON  ETBA
DYKES LONG  SEAR
```

PUZZLE 12

```
  BLBA   HELPER
 MAUER  AHEATER
TARGET PRISTINE
ERRORS EARS  CGI
AGE   BASE  SKIN
MORA BARS  BEEF
STAR ALL  LOTTO
  MGMT BOOT
STROS BUS  LARD
CRUD SUDS  ERIE
GRUB CONS   RPF
YES  BERT STRIKE
RETREATS  SEAVER
ONEBASE   BRIAN
 SEATED  CALL
```

PUZZLE 13

```
M A T A . A L A S . L O A D S
A N E W . C O M P . A N N I E
S T E A L H O M E . S H O R T
S I N G L E T O N . T E N T H
. . N B A . . T E R A .
. T H E I T C H . C O R B I N
P O O R . E R I C . S T A T E
A T L . R O M A N . . S E T
W A L S H . P O K E . D I M S
S L A T O N . M E T R I C S .
. I T C H . . W A S .
B B P C T . A B S O R B I N G
A L I K E . Y O U R E A B U M
T U N E S . E R I K . N L M B
H E A R T . S E T S . D A B A
```

PUZZLE 14

```
S L U R . H E A T . A L O T
E O N E . B E R T H . D E U S
M A I N . I R A T E . M A S K
I N T E N S E . A S S I S T S
. W O O D . C H A S E S .
N B D . N I C H O L S .
B E A M . S A L . W E I G H T
H A B I T . O . S O L I S
F R A S O R . T B O . N A D A
. S T E P H A N . D E R
. A L C A L A . R I B S .
S M A L L E R . C O M P O S E
D A T A . A K R O N . A T T N
B Y E S . S E E D S . S T U D
C A R S . E D G E . M O B S
```

PUZZLE 15

```
B C B L . A L P B . S T A T S
A L A B . C O L A . H E A R T
S O I L . E V A N . A A A B A
I N T . R E S T A U R A N T
C E S S A . T E N N .
. B A R R E R A . C G L
T W O H O U R . H . S H O E
P E A R S O N . T E S T I N G
A R I Z . T . F A I L I N G
S A T . F R A N M I L .
. F O A M . P E T C O
C O N F I R M I N G . H O U
B B A L L . B L U R . L I D S
M E T A L . L I T E . B R E T
C R E W S . E A S Y . A D D S
```

PUZZLE 16

```
G R S L . A M B L . A S H E D
R O L E . P I P E . S T I L E
E S I X . P L A N . H A Y E S
E S P I N A L . S E T B A C K
N O S C O R E . E A R .
. O V E R . S T E N G A L
. F I N A L . S E R I A L
P E P . . S A C
P E O P L E . P A S T A .
A D D R E S S . C O N N .
. T B C . A R T I S T S
A L L S T A R . S T E P H A N
A L I N E . A M I R . P O L O
A B E A R . P I N A . E V E R
S I N G S . E D G Y . T E S T
```

PUZZLE 17

	P	A	S	T		C	O	B	B		S	N	A	G
W	A	C	H	A		A	G	R	O		C	O	R	E
O	N	A	I	R		G	L	A	D		H	O	T	N
B	E	L	L			B	E	E	S		D	E	N	S	E
A	L	L	D	A	Y				S	T	U	D		
		T	W	E	E	T			B	O	U	G	H	T
G	A	S			A	S	S	E	S	S		L	A	I	R
D	A	I	S	Y		B	A	D		B	E	R	T	I
B	B	B	A		G	A	M	B	L	E		B	S	M
C	A	L	L	E	R		S	C	O	T	T			
		A	Y	B	L				U	S	A	B	L	E
S	C	A	R	E		A	B	A	D		G	O	A	D
C	A	L	I		B	U	L	L		Y	O	U	N	G
A	L	O	E		F	E	U	D		B	U	N	D	Y
B	L	T	S		P	R	E	S		L	T	D	S	

PUZZLE 18

S	P	B	L		S	O	A	P		G	B	L	
S	C	A	R	E		A	N	C	E		B	L	I	P
T	O	T	E	N		N	E	A	T		G	O	A	L
A	R	I	A	S		T	I	M	E	R		W		A
B	E	N	S		S	A	L	E		E	S	S	A	Y
	R	O	T	T	E	N		R	E	P	L	A	C	E
			A	A	A		A	R	R	I	V	E	D
	D	R	O	P	S			R	I	D	E	S	
H	E	A	D	N	O	D		D	A	N			
I	N	T	O	O	N	E		E	N	T	I	C	E
S	T	I	R	S		L	I	F	T		C	H	A	S
S		O		E	H	I	R	E		C	O	A	S	T
E	O	N	E		I	V	A	N		A	N	N	I	E
D	I	A	L		N	E	T	S		B	I	C	E	P
L	L	B		T	R	E	E		A	C	E	R	

PUZZLE 19

	S	L	A	P		S	T	A	N	D	S	
	M	A	I	L	E		T	A	V	E	R	A	S
T	A	N	N	E	R		M	O	T	I	V	A	T	E
O	N	D	E	C	K		O	W	E	D		W	I	N
M	T	L			O	V	E	R		L	A	S	T
A	L	O	T		S	H	E	D		T	U	R	F
S	E	T	H		K	I	D		T	O	M	M	Y
		A	L	S	O		B	A	T	B			
	S	T	I	C	H		T	A	P		E	S	B	A
	T	O	S	S		M	A	S	S		R	E	A	L
B	O	B	S		C	O	P	S			A	L	T
I	R	A		G	A	L	E		S	E	T	T	L	E
R	I	C	H	A	R	D	S		O	P	E	N	E	R
D	E	C	E	I	V	E		A	B	L	U	R	
	S	O	R	T	E	D		P	A	L	M		

PUZZLE 20

	R	O	B	E	R	T	S		P	I	N	A
B	A	L		L	O	O	T		U	S	A	B
I	N	I	T	I	A	T	O	R		M	A	T	A
N	O	V	A		D	E	M	O		P	A	I	N	T
D	U	E	L		N	A	B		C	O	D	Y
S	T	R	E	A	M		C	L	A	P		N	A	P
		N	B	A		H	E	L	L		A	G	E
	H	A	T	E	I	T		S	T	A	B	L	E
C	O	P		A	L	A	B		E	T	A	
U	M	P		R	E	N	O		R	E	N	D	E	R
T	E	L	E		A	N	A		N	A	D	A
S	T	E	V	E		N	I	C	K		O	M	I	T
	O	P	E	N		A	L	T	E	R	N	A	T	E
W	I	N	D		L	O	N	E		G	O	D
N	E	T	S		A	R	O	S	T	E	R

PUZZLE 21

S	K	S	H		C	A	L	C		F	I	E	R	S
T	A	C	O		O	B	E	Y		E	R	N	I	E
A	A	A	S		W	R	A	A		M	O	O	S	E
N	I	N	E	T	E	E	N		J	A	N	S	E	N
		U	N	U	S	U	A	L						
S	T	A	K	E	S		P	R	E	D	A	T	E	
T	I	R	E	S		C	A	S	E		A	R	E	A
R	E	I	N		C	O	D	E	D		T	I	N	G
O	U	S	T		L	O	S	T		L	E	A	S	E
S	P	E	A	K	E	R		L	E	S	S	E	R	
	H	A	S	B	E	E	N							
F	R	Y	M	A	N		A	H	A	S	B	E	E	N
A	B	A	L	L		O	D	I	N		L	A	T	E
W	I	L	L	I		A	G	R	O		A	S	B	A
N	S	S	B	L		K	E	E	N		B	E	L	T

PUZZLE 22

	S	W	A	P		F	L	O	R	E	S
	M	A	I	L	E		R	E	G	U	L	A	R
T	A	N	N	E	R		D	I	A	L	N	I	N	E
O	N	D	E	C	K		R	E	N	E		E	T	A
M	T	L		B	E	N	S		T	S	A	R		
A	L	O	T		A	B	A	D		T	H	E	N	
S	E	T	H		B	S	M		P	A	R	R	A	
	R	I	C	A		C	A	P	E					
P	L	U	G	S		P	H	P		A	R	M	S	
L	O	S	S		K	A	A	I		T	E	A	M	
C	A	S	T		P	A	I	N		V	I	A		
E	Y	E		D	A	N	G		T	H	R	I	L	L
R	E	S	P	O	N	S	E		R	A	I	S	E	L
T	R	I	P	L	E	A		E	N	D	E	D		
S	T	A	L	L	S		A	G	E	D				

PUZZLE 23

O	S	B	A		C	Z	A	R		A	P	A	I	R
M	E	A	N		H	O	L	E		L	E	A	S	E
I	G	N	O	R	A	N	C	E		A	A	A	B	A
T	A	S	T	E	L	E	S	S		B	R	A	N	D
	H	A	M		E	R	A	S						
T	H	E	M	E	S	S		S	M	O	O	T	H	
P	O	O	R		R	E	P	S		A	N	N	I	E
A	T	L		S	T	E	A	M		E	R	A		
W	A	L	S	H		S	E	M	I		D	I	E	T
S	L	A	T	O	N		D	E	T	A	I	L	S	
	I	T	C	H		C	W	S						
B	B	P	C	T		O	N	E	H	O	P	P	E	R
A	L	I	K	E		S	A	T	E	L	L	I	T	E
T	U	N	E	S		E	M	B	L		A	P	B	A
H	E	A	R	T		D	E	A	L		Y	E	L	L

PUZZLE 24

G	A	P	S		C	A	L	C		N	A	L	B
U	N	I	T		A	L	I	A	R		A	R	E	A
A	C	T	A		C	O	M	B	O		T	R	A	Y
M	E	T	R	I	C	S		A	C	T	I	O	N	S
	T	R	E	E		T	H	R	O	W	S			
P	S	P		P	R	E	T	E	E	N				
E	P	I	C		T	S	N		T	E	A	R	I	T
R	U	N	O	N		O		S	L	I	C	E		
K	R	E	M	E	R		L	L	B		S	B	B	A
	P	R	E	M	I	E	R			S	A	M		
D	E	R	I	V	E		T	E	A	R				
D	E	V	I	S	E	D		T	A	V	E	R	A	S
A	C	E	S		R	I	D	E	S		C	O	D	I
B	O	N	E		S	N	O	R	T		A	L	O	T
A	R	T	S		E	A	T	S		P	E	T	E	

109

PUZZLE 25

S	C	A	R		A	P	P	T		R	E	C	A	P
C	O	B	A		S	O	L	E		A	R	O	M	A
O	V	E	N		S	L	A	P		L	I	N	E	D
P	E	A		N	O	S	E	B	L	E	E	D	S	
E	R	R	O	R			T	R	A	Y				
		R	O	W	S	E	A	T			T	B	C	
	P	R	E	M	I	E	R		T		S	E	A	L
A	L	T	O	O	N	A		M	I	S	T	A	K	E
B	O	B	S		D		R	U	N	H	O	M	E	
L	Y	B			S	T	A	G	G	E	R			
			G	O	O	D			D	E	N	T	S	
F	A	T	H	E	R	T	I	M	E			A	R	I
A	N	S	O	N		A	C	B	L		A	P	E	N
S	T	A	K	E		L	A	C	E		A	B	A	G
T	I	R	E	S		K	L	A	C		A	L	D	S

PUZZLE 26

A	G	E	D		E	T	C	H		C	L	O	T	H
R	O	S	E		S	E	G	A		H	I	G	H	A
O	O	P	S		T	R	B	N		E	F	L	I	N
A	S	Y	S	T	E	M		S	C	R	E	E	N	S
R	E	S	E	R	V	E		E	L	I				
			R	E	A	D		L	O	S	M	E	T	S
	T	O	T	E	N				T	H	R	O	W	N
B	O	B									N	I	B	
O	L	E	R	U	D			C	O	H	E	N		
O	L	Y	M	P	I	C		D	A	T	A			
			E	R	A		E	M	B	R	A	C	E	
G	A	R	D	N	E	R		D	E	A	D	R	E	D
B	L	O	O	D		P	O	U	R		H	A	N	G
S	C	O	P	E		E	B	C	A		A	N	T	E
A	S	K	E	D		T	R	E	S		T	O	S	S

PUZZLE 27

	T	A	K	E		P	A	L	M		O	S	B	A
D	E	L	A	Y		A	L	O	T		B	E	E	R
E	N	I	N	E		G	O	A	L		S	A	L	T
E	T	A	S		F	E	E	D		P	O	T	T	S
P	H	R	A	S	E			S	B	B	L			
		S	W	E	E	P		B	R	E	W	E	R	
B	F	J		A	T	T	A	C	K		T	I	C	E
B	R	E	T	T		B	O	O		B	E	T	T	S
B	A	S	H		S	A	L	I	V	A		T	B	T
A	T	T	I	R	E		O	N	A	I	R			
		E	A	T	S			S	L	I	D	E	R	
R	A	L	L	Y		A	S	S	T		V	E	R	Y
S	L	O	B		P	I	C	S		N	E	V	I	N
V	I	S	A		B	L	A	B		B	R	I	C	E
P	E	E	R		A	S	B	A		D	A	N	K	

PUZZLE 28

	S	H	O	P		A	M	B	L		O	F	F	
A	C	U	N	A		C	O	R	Y		B	A	A	B
H	O	M	E	R		A	R	U	N		P	I	N	A
O	R	B	I	T		M	A	I	N	E		R		R
Y	E	L	L		B	E	N	S		A	S	F	A	N
	S	E	L	L	E	R		E	A	R	H	O	L	E
			A	N	A		S	T	L	O	U	I	S	
	S	T	A	N	D			T	I	T	L	E		
U	P	E	N	D	E	D		P	I	E				
S	I	N	C	E	R	E		A	R	R	E	S	T	
E	N	D	E	R		L	U	R	E		N	E	A	T
S		T		S	H	A	P	E		S	T	I	L	E
I	P	O	D		E	Y	E	D		P	I	Z	E	R
T	E	B	A		R	E	N	E		U	R	E	N	A
	P	E	D		O	D	D	S		R	E	S	T	

PUZZLE 29

```
S S B A   A F F O R D
  S T E A L   B E A T O U T
H A R A S S   F R A C T U R E
A L O N S O   R E S T   G A L
Y U M     C O A T   W H B L
E T A S   S I N K   P A U L
S E N T   A T T   S W I P E
    A B F I   B E R T
A R I S E   S I T   E R A S
M A R V   L I D S   D E L T
L E N S   J O G S   T B A
O R G   P A W N   S C O R E R
T I E G A M E S   P A P E R S
S C R A P E S   C L E A T
  A S S I S T   T I N T
```

PUZZLE 30

```
  T A R   O D D S   C O M B
S O R E   R A N T   A V I L A
S T O P   I N F O   N E C B L
B A L L O O N   R E T R E A T
C L E A N L Y   E X S
    C U E   E E I G H T
  P R E S S   S E R G I O
O B A       B C W
R E C E S S   C R A N K
G O E S T O   H O T
    A B N   W E A T H E R
A G A I N S T   A C R E A G E
B L U N T   B A S K   M U G S
L O T T O   S I T E   P L O T
  B O O N   A M E D   T S N
```

PUZZLE 31

```
A B A D   A B E D   A S H E D
B A M A   T R A P   B L A D E
A B E T   B E G S   B U L G E
G E N E R A T E   S O R T E D
    A T T R A C T
A R A M I S   B O T T L E S
L O C A L   S H O T   E O N E
P L A Y   S H O U T   A S I A
H E R O   T A F T   T R E N T
A N D R O I D   M E S S E S
    P R E S S E R
C A L V E S   P A R A L L E L
O N I O N   A I B C   L I V E
S T A T E   T R E E   B E E N
T I M E R   T E R R   I N N S
```

PUZZLE 32

```
  T E R A   A T T A C K
  C R A I G   T H E S H O W
S O U R C E   A T O M B A L L
T O S S E D   L I M P   S A L
A L T     T I R E   H E R B
F E E T   D U K E   G O R E
F R E E   O N E   F R I S K
    R Y N E   S U D S
G A M E S   B O S   T S K S
A G E S   W A R S   S A N O
C R U D   M O S T   M I L
A R I   H O M E   S H R E V E
R E L I E V E S   L E A D E R
S T A R L I N   U R I A S
T R A D E S   R E L Y
```

PUZZLE 33

```
TSAR  PPBA  MORAN
BABE  HERD  AVILA
ABANDONED   RECAP
ALTERNATE   CROSS
   WEE     DIES
 DRAWARM  PLEASE
MAUL PEAK  LEFTY
INN  PETIT   TIE
SCOOP DELI  BENS
TENURE  STEWART
   TEST   BAT
GLASS  UNWRITTEN
ELVIS  NINETEAMS
ABIDE  ECBA  RTBB
RIDER  SOCK  YELL
```

PUZZLE 34

```
 ADS  HSBB  NABL
SHOE  REPO  ONAIR
CONN  DEAN  MAINE
BLOATED   DRILLED
LETTERS  SUN
   ORB    TEJADA
 ARRAY   HERMAN
KBO        ETA
AFLOAT   ARENA
NIEKRO    BAL
    ROB  ARTISTS
URSHELA  BASEHIT
BASES  BLAH  SODA
ATBAT  IBLA  EVEN
 EATS  PALM  RES
```

PUZZLE 35

```
PPBA  CIGS  RAMOS
ALOU  OREL  ALINE
CEOS  DONE  LANCE
KAN  INTERESTED
STEAM   IVEY
  CIRCLES   CBO
 BARCODE P GOAT
JAMESON  PEDROIA
OILS  T RECEIPT
NLB   FRONTAL
   TOES   NLMOY
FISHERCATS  ANA
ABEAR  AREA  LIES
BLAIR  LIEN  ALIE
CARRY  LONG  BELL
```

PUZZLE 36

```
CPBL  SHOT  CALEB
HOLA  WABA  OLIVA
AWAY  ENCY  NOTES
REMOTES  LETTERS
TREVINO   ONE
   EVEN  RONALDO
 ALROY   STREET
WBO        ASB
ALOMAR   PLUNK
RETIRED  PREP
   RIO  LEADING
PRESENT  APPAREL
LACES  COCA  TACO
ATBAT  OBER  ETBA
YEARS  MADE  DELT
```

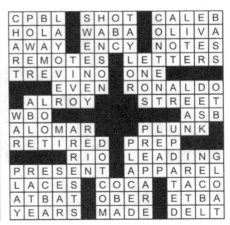

PUZZLE 37

```
  C H I P   C A L B   O S B L
B O O N E   A L O U   B O R E
A L I K E   G O A D   S U E S
B O S S   F E E D   J O L T S
E N T I R E   S B B L
    T O T A L   O N E E N D
A P R   S A L I V A   T A P E
R O O F S   I S O   Z E R P A
T S A R   S E T T L E   N B L
S T R I P E   S H I R T
    E A T S   F O R M A L
C H A N T   E A S E   I C B A
H O L D   G V B A   T A R I K
A N A L   B E A K   B L A R E
S E B Y   A N T E   U S E D
```

PUZZLE 38

```
N P B L   P A L M   W A G E R
G O A O   N B B A   C A R V E
B L T S   C B C C   G R O I N
L O S E   O A K   O G L E
    S N O T   A M E N
S B R   A N T U N A   S E A
L U E T G E   S I T   S T A N
A L A B   B L U N T   H A T E
N L C S   A A A   H O R T O N
G S H   S U L S E R   E N D
    S E E N   C W B L
D B A T   C A R   A C R E
A L T E R   H A U L   S H O T
L E A V E   E B B A   S O S A
E D G E S   D A B A   O W E S
```

PUZZLE 39

```
  S A L E   O F F E R S
M I N O R   P R O L O N G
T A N A N A   A P A R I C I O
A N G L E S   F O N T   K P B
B A L   R I S K   D I P S
L E E R   A B L E   T R E E
E A S E   H I M   H O I S T
  C E O S   W A B L
A L E X Y   F A R   L C B A
M E S S   F O R D   S H A M
B E T S   G O R Y   E L B
A R T   P A R K   O R A C L E
T I E G A M E S   M I C K E R
S C R A P E S   A S H E D
A S S I S T   R E E D
```

PUZZLE 40

```
  A T T   A B L E   T R A Y
G U R U   L O A N   R E R U N
A T A G   L O G O   U N C L E
L O N G E S T   L O S E S I T
A S S I S T S   I N T
    N B A   U E H A R A
  S U G A R   S E R I E S
C A N       M N B
B L I M P S   G H O S T
A T T I R E   R A N
    O B A   W A V E C A P
P I N E T A R   E Y E B A L L
S P A C E   O W E S   A N T E
P O T T S   M E M O   S H E A
D E B T   A S S N   E A R
```

PUZZLE 41

```
KAAI    ACSB    LISTS
ISBN    BOOM    ISAAC
LIFT    BULL    MANTA
TAILBONE    SINGER
    ATTRACT
ACCOST      POSTWAR
TRANS   GOAT    AIDE
BUNT    HABIT   TREE
ASBA    OMAR    REELS
THEPINE     HURDLE
    BULLPEN
THOMAS      AHASBEEN
RODON   SNOT    ORBA
AMOVE   ACNE    SIBL
PEREZ   LEER    SCAB
```

PUZZLE 42

```
    CTBA    ASPASM
    BOSOX   SHELTER
SENATE      FOOTLINE
HATRED   LURE   CDN
ONE     MINT    SHOE
GENE    SAND    BAEZ
ODDS    ORG     CESSA
    CORK    BONA
SCOPE   BBL     KABC
CARS    RBSA    IBLA
RANT    SEGA    UER
INT     WMBU    GOALIE
ONSCREEN    ANGLES
TEEBALL     STEER
DECALS      POST
```

PUZZLE 43

```
BANS    ETCH    CLASE
ABLE    NWBI    HAGER
SEBASTIAN    ARENA
STARLIN     THRUST
    CUT     SETS
SCHMIDT     RESIGN
BTF     PEARL   RADIO
OIL     STATS   INT
BEARD   ADDED   OTB
SBPERC      ESPORTS
    PILE    ANA
CALLED      FRONTAL
TOTAL   GREATDAME
BRICE   ABAT    OPEN
TAPED   RATE    MENS
```

PUZZLE 44

```
    TBC     ANTE    TRAY
AREA    CAIN    RERUN
BARN    AMMO    UNCLE
AIRTIME     LOSESIT
GLASSES     INT
    EAR     UEHARA
ARENA   SERIES
NAB         MNB
SAINTS      GHOST
BADHOP      LAP
    RIM     WAVECAP
ALBERTO     OVERALL
BOONE   YIMI    ASIA
RUNON   EVEN    TENN
PASS    RYNE    EYE
```

PUZZLE 45

```
F C T B   G T B L   A D A P T
A A A A   R O L E   L O S E S
C N B L   I R O N   I N S T A
E B L     N E W S C A S T E R
T E E T H     S E A R
    H O T T E S T   C A B
  P E R Y E A R   C   W O B A
P I N E T A R   C H E A P E R
A N C E   R   A B U L L E T
S A Y     S C R A P E S
    P I L E   C H E S S
T H R E A T E N E D   N E T
H E A R N   N A M E   S O L E
E R N I E   C D B L   S L I P
Y O K E L   H O L T   B I G S
```

PUZZLE 46

```
C H O P   T R A Y   O N T A P
L I N E   W I N E   B O W I E
A C E R   O V A L   S L I D E
S K U N K   A L L S E A T E R
E S P I N A L   O H R
    N E T S   W A V E C A P
  S W E E T     W E A L T H
B A A           A A A
S M I T H S   C H A N G
M E T R I C S   S H O T
    S A W   C O L L I N S
D R A F T B E E R   T A S T E
R A D I O   A R E A   N B B A
A R O A R   T I E R   T E S T
G E T T Y   S E N T   A L A S
```

PUZZLE 47

```
  H I K E   A B C S   G E M S
M O R A N   P A L E   A T I P
S T A N D   B R E W   L B C A
B E T S   L C B A   A L L E N
P L E A S E   N B B A
  S P E C S   U N R E A L
M E T   C R O W D S   D A L E
B R E T T   S E E   M O T I F
F I S H   S T E E L E   S E T
A C T I V E   T R E E S
  E B C A   S T I T C H
A B A L L   M E S S   E R I E
M U S B   W A B L   A R E N A
P T B A   B L B A   T R A C T
S T A R   F L A P   M A T H
```

PUZZLE 48

```
C U E S   E C T B   L O G O S
A S S T   R O A R   A R O M A
S A B R   A U T O   D E V I N
T B A A     R E S   O T T O
    W A R S   S P O S
M A P   P E E W E E   R B F
A L L A R D   Y A N   C A L I
R O A D   S H A U N   A L A S
C A T S   F A T   A L B E R T
O N E   A N T U N A   Y E S
  S A N D   S T A B
C H A T   I C E   A C N E
L A C E D   C B S B   S O R T
A L T E R   A S I A   I C B A
Y E A R S   P I T T   C A B S
```

PUZZLE 49

	F	A	C	T		G	A	P	P	E	R	
R	A	D	I	O		E	L	I	E	S	E	R
D	E	V	O	T	E		S	T	I	L	E	T	T	O
A	D	O	N	I	S		H	O	N	E		E	R	A
U	E	R		C	O	L	E		O	V	E	R
E	Y	E	D		C	O	R	D		W	R	A	A
R	E	D	O		B	P	T		P	A	I	N	T
	O	N	U	S		B	E	R	G	
S	C	M	B	A		F	L	D		I	S	A	N
H	O	E	D		L	I	E	S		N	I	D	O
H	E	R	D		S	O	L	D		N	E	V
O	L	D		S	L	A	M		M	U	S	C	L	E
S	T	E	R	O	I	D	S		A	P	P	E	A	L
S	E	R	V	I	C	E		S	T	O	R	Y
	R	O	L	L	E	D		H	O	S	E	

PUZZLE 50

	L	B	A		R	U	N	S		A	C	R	E
R	E	A	M		A	R	E	A		S	H	O	C	K
E	A	S	E		N	G	B	L		P	A	S	T	A
A	V	E	R	A	G	E		A	B	I	D	E	B	Y
D	E	C	I	D	E	D		D	E	R	
	C	A	R			A	I	M	T	H	E
A	D	A	M	S		U	N	R	E	A	L
L	A	A			L	Y	B
L	A	B	A	T	T		T	R	I	E	S
C	A	S	T	R	O		A	B	N
	A	U	S		A	V	I	S	A	I	L
T	H	E	D	I	R	T		G	E	S	T	U	R	E
A	A	R	O	N		E	V	E	R		E	T	A	S
P	R	I	M	E		P	I	N	A		A	R	T	S
D	E	E	D		S	E	T	S		D	Y	E

CONGRATULATIONS
YOU FINISHED

Made in the USA
Monee, IL
17 September 2024

65978858R00066